How to Generate Highly Profitable Google Ads

Discover the Key Method to Explode Your Clicks and Conversions Using Google AdWords

By reading this document, the reader agrees that under no circumstances is the author responsible for any losses, direct or indirect, that are incurred as a result of the use of information contained within this document, including, but not limited to, errors, omissions, or inaccuracies.

Table of Contents

Introduction

The internet is awash with strategies to make money. A common theme among all of these strategies is the need to make yourself heard and to stand out from the rest of the pack. Indeed, if you're not showing off what you're about these days, you might as well not exist.

Setting aside the sociological aspects of such an environment, there is no denying that advertising is a necessity in today's digital business landscape. Well, I say digital, but business landscape is more accurate since all businesses live online anyway, and even brick and mortar ones cannot afford to not have an online presence.

Yes, indeed, the days of "Build it and they will come" are long gone. You need to stand out both in terms of your product as well as your marketing strategy. The rise of the internet as an avenue for business has turned the marketing field upside down.

What used to be a field heavily focused on generating buzzwords and psychology has now become such that its practitioners need to understand the value of things like data analytics and platform specific advertising. The digital landscape is large, and there is no shortage of methods to advertise.

Not all forms of advertising requires spending. The beauty of the internet is that it has made spreading word of mouth reviews a lot easier, and this has manifested itself as the inbound marketing field. Over the long run, inbound marketing works and is what will generate huge profits for your business.

Inbound Versus Outbound

There is a slight hitch when it comes to inbound marketing, though: it takes time. Lots of it. Depending on the niche you're in, it might take close to a decade to make an impact. So should you sit tight all that while calmly focusing on classic inbound tactics such as SEO and content generation? Well, you should be doing that as routine anyway.

However, understand that to run a business successfully you owe it to yourself and your employees to generate profits as soon as possible. For all of the low cost and organic growth that inbound marketing gives you, it simply doesn't work as a sole marketing strategy. You need outbound marketing to boost your efforts initially.

Outbound marketing refers to running ads on digital platforms such as Facebook and Google. Facebook is the most famous one and has an ad console that seems deliberately designed to confuse the hell out of anyone using it. Facebook's reach as a social network puts advertisers on its platform at its complete mercy, and they have to accept its evils if they wish to play.

This is in stark contrast to Google and its ad network. Google does not invade the personal space of its readers as Facebook does. What I mean is, think back to when you saw an ad on Facebook. You were probably doing something else and suddenly in your feed, an ad popped up distracting you.

Ads on Facebook need to be extremely catchy and often people end up clicking on them just to see what they're about without any intention of buying the product. This is a waste of a click.

Google ads have an in-built advantage in that search intent has already been filtered for.

In other words, the person searching for stuff on Google has pretty much given a green light to advertisers that they wish to receive ads since they're explicitly searching for solutions to what they're looking for. This is a massive advantage. There's another advantage as well that inbound marketing fundamentalists tend to ignore.

Activity and Organic Rank

Running successful Google ads improves your organic rankings on Google search. This is because Google places a high degree of importance on relevance and usefulness. If the people clicking onto your product page stay there for a while and if the number of clicks keep increasing over time, Google figures out that your page is actually quite valuable.

Thus, when someone searches for your keyword (I'll explain this later if you don't understand it fully right now), Google gives you the one-two punch of showing your ad as well as showcasing your web page in the organic search results. This is a win-win! Thus, your outbound marketing efforts help your inbound marketing and can get you to hit exponential growth sooner!

Is it all good news, though? Well, nothing ever is. The truth is that Google ads can be hard to crack, especially given the sophistication of the competition that is around. You need a guide that can show you the ropes in a practical and step by step manner. The reality is that there's a lot of stuff within Google's platform, and the data you are provided can get you to lose yourself within it easily.

What you need to do is to approach all of this information logically and to then align it with your overall content strategy. You might be wondering at this point, is it worth doing all of this if you're a small business?

Small Businesses Unite!

Here's the thing: Google loves small businesses! In fact, when people search for stuff online, Google takes the location into account and displays relevant results that are nearby. The search results page is explicitly designed for this. Go ahead and search for a pizza place near you. What will you see in the ads on top of the page?

Chances are you'll see the usual suspects like Domino's or Pizza Hut, but right below them is usually a space reserved for the local pizza place. You too can compete with national brands since Google ads are a great leveler. This isn't just the case with local searches.

Even global searches have the ability to showcase your business in the ads section. If you can nail down your keywords, then the sky's the limit. At once, you have access to the entire world of people searching for your product! This beats having to constantly interrupt people's routines on Facebook and convince them to check you out.

This is why the ROI on Google campaigns tend to be a lot higher when compared with Facebook campaigns. Both in terms of organic search as well as advertising ROI, Google will put you far ahead. What you need to now do is take the time to really digest the things I'm going to teach you.

This book aims to have you running profitable ad campaigns once you're done reading and understanding the material within it. Some of this stuff is easy. Some of it is complicated. However, don't let the large amounts of information intimidate you. Once you understand them, you'll do it yourself easily.

So now that we're clear on what you need to do and what I'm going to give you in return, let's dive right in!

Chapter 1: How AdWords Works

Google's advertising program called AdWords is its most profitable product and, frankly, it isn't even close (Patel, 2017). They must be doing something right if so many people around the world are willing to spend money on this thing. AdWords as a concept is not unique but just like Google does with search, it is the best executed ad network there is.

In this chapter, I'm going to walk you through the basics of AdWords style networks and how they work. To understand how to be successful, understanding the format of this type of advertising is crucial. So let's take a look.

Pay Per Click

AdWords is a performance based ad network, like every other advertising platform on the internet. This means that you're not paying for an advertising spot. Instead, you're paying for a particular action to be carried out. The action you pay Google for is a click. Hence the term pay per click or PPC ads.

The way it works is quite simple. Each of your ads target a particular keyword or phrase and when a person searches for this phrase, your ad shows up. If they click on it, you get charged a certain amount and Google transfers the person to your website or landing page. Simple, right?

This is in direct contrast to how advertising has traditionally worked in the newspaper or magazines and such. Over there, you're paying to rent space in their publication upfront while you have no way or tracking the efficacy of your campaigns. You could include a code in your ads of some sort, but even those methods are pretty tough to measure.

PPC ads have no such problems and therefore enable you to focus like a laser on just the things that are working for you and invest more there. Google helps you out with all of this thanks to the mountain of data they provide you with. The first thing for you to understand is the mechanics of how Google decides which ads to show first and in what order.

Auction

The AdWords market for a keyword is an auction. Various advertisers place bids, and Google selects whose ads to display. At least this is how it used to be when AdWords was first rolled out. As you can imagine, this system favors those with deep pockets quite heavily since they could simply outbid the rest of the competition quite easily.

What's more, there was another flaw in the algorithm in that advertisers could bid for any keyword imaginable. Therefore, if you searched for a popular movie's reviews you could have been shown ads for a dishwasher on top of the page. Understandably, this sort of thing provides a poor experience to those browsing, and Google fixed all of this with a simple metric.

This metric is called the Quality Score, and all of your campaigns should be designed with this in mind. The Q score is a great leveler for advertisers of all sizes since it minimizes the effect of big budgets and brand name recognition. If your Q score happens to be higher than that of a far larger competitor, your ad can be listed above theirs. How great is that?

This is not to say that the amount of money you bid doesn't matter. Far from it. It's just that the ad placement is determined by the combination of the Q score and your bid, which gives you a far better chance of duking it out with the big boys. Before we get into looking at how the quality score is determined, though, I need to bring you up to speed on some jargon.

First we have the term "impressions." This is simply the number of times your ad was displayed when people searched for that relevant keyword. In other words, how many people saw this ad? There could be multiple views in there, but generally impressions are a pretty good metric to estimate your ads' reach.

When a person clicks on your ad you get charged, as I mentioned earlier. Dividing the number of clicks by the impressions gives you a percentage called the Click Through Rate or CTR. This is one of the huge metrics in PPC ads, so keep this in mind.

So now you're paying for your ads, what is the cost you're incurring for simply displaying those ads? Well, this is what the Cost Per Mille or CPM is. The CPM is the amount you've spent (thanks to people clicking on your ads) per thousand impressions. Now that we've got this out of the way, let's get back to the auction house.

When you setup your campaign for keywords, you will need to fix a budget and a bid. Google exists to make money, so naturally, it is going to favor those who bid more, assuming all else is equal. What if you're the highest bidder by a mile? Well, Google won't charge you the entire amount because it optimizes for the bid size with regard to impressions.

My point is that you won't always be spending the exact bid amount. You won't spend more than that amount for sure. AdWords campaigns run on autopilot, and you fix a maximum budget per day. Successful advertisers spend a small amount up front testing various keywords and then scale the ones that are successful into larger campaigns.

The second half of the ad placement puzzle is the Q score. Every ad you run will have a Q score assigned to it by Google; the higher the better. What are the factors that go into determining the Q score?

Quality Scores

Briefly, here are the things that Google takes into account:

1. Relevance

2. CTR

3. Account history

4. Landing page bounce

Relevance is simply an internal score each keyword is given with regard to what the user is searching. For example, if someone searches for "best laptop accessory," a keyword such as "best smartphone accessory" is not as relevant as "best external hard drives" and so on. Therefore, it is very important that when you setup your keywords, you need to make them relevant to what your customers might search for.

The next factor is the CTR. Simply put, how effective is your ad when it comes to people clicking on it? The higher the CTR, the more Google respects your ad since this is clearly more relevant to the audience than your competitors' ads. Interestingly, as your account gets older, Google will project your past CTRs into the future and if they're good, you might even get a head start.

This is what the account history is all about. The longer you've been doing this, the better Google can determine whether you actually know what you're doing. If you're good at it, your new ads will start off with the same effective CTR (as projected by Google) as your old ads despite not having received any clicks. This is not a huge factor, but it does make a difference if you're good at designing high CTR ads. The other factor within the account history metric is whether you actually sell good products or if you're espousing something fraudulent.

The last factor is a very important one and refers to what happens when people click on your ad and view your landing page. If they tend to immediately leave the page and go back to Google, this is called a bounce. The lower the bounce rate, the more relevant your ad and thus the higher your Q score is going to be.

This is why the design of your landing page needs to be clean and easy to navigate. If the user gets confused or doesn't get a good idea of what's going on, they're likely to bounce and Google will penalize you for this. All of these factors are taken together, along with your maximum bid, and Google spits out a metric called the AdRank.

The calculation is straightforward. It is simply the product of your Q score and your maximum bid. Now here's the nerdy bit. Before deciding to display your ad, Google takes the Q score, your bid and your AdRank into account and then decides how much you should pay per click. This is called your Cost Per Click or CPC.

Your CPC is therefore not necessarily all about your maximum bid. If your quality score is high enough, you will end up paying less and have your ad shown higher than your competitor who bids far more than you. Your CPC is your profit indicator since it literally tells you how much you're paying for a click and you can compare this directly to your profit margins.Get too many useless clicks and you'll end up wasting money.

You will need to constantly monitor your campaigns since it is easy for spending to get out of hand. In fact, let's look at budgetary concerns now.

Budgeting

Remember that you're not running ads for a charity. Your ultimate aim with these ads is to make money. Therefore, your end goal should always be to sell a product or a service, which will help you recoup your money quickly. This might sound unbelievable, but there are a lot of companies that spend tons of money on AdWords only to have people fill out a form that indicates interest or sign up for some low commitment email list.

This is a surefire way to lose money since daily costs can add up no matter how low your maximum daily limit is. Therefore, always keep your end goal in mind when designing your campaigns. The key metric to measure here is your conversions. The CTR is one half of that since it indicates how many people are clicking onto your website or product page.

Thankfully, figuring out your ad budget is simple. You start by defining your profit margins. Let's say you earn $10 per sale in profit. Next, you need to estimate a conversion rate. This is different from the CTR, which is the number of people who click your ad. Here, I'm talking about the number of people who buy your product once they land on your page. A decent number to shoot for, if you haven't done any sort of PPC ads before is 1%. So one out of every ten will buy your product.

Every click you receive is coming from Google, so you'll need to pay them. So how much of your profit are you willing to spend on ads? Is $3 (30%) fine? Is it $5 (50%)? And so on. Remember to take your other costs into account as well before deciding on this number. Multiply all of these together, and you will get your Max CPC or the maximum amount you can pay per click to maintain your margins.

Max CPC= $10*0.01*0.3 = 0.03 per click. (profit*conversion rate*percentage of gross profit spent on ads)

Now, with this in hand, you can determine what your maximum budget should be. Remember that you should test your ads first to see if these assumptions hold. Therefore, aim for a small campaign to generate a few clicks and once you receive some data, you can focus more on the keywords that work and spend more on them for better results.

An ideal time period to test is 10 days. Let's say you will receive twenty clicks per day, which is a realistic number. Of course, this depends on your niche but this is a good average across niches. So your per day maximum spend is:

Max CPC * Number of clicks = $0.03*20 = 0.60 per day.

Total Budget for 10 days = $0.6*10 = 6

If you want to run it for 30 days then your budget will be $18 and so on. Now that you have a handle on your budget, let's look at how you can enhance performance via bidding strategies and the options Google gives you.

Bidding and Modifiers

When you setup your campaign, Google is going to give you a bunch of options when it comes to the management of your bids. When starting out, I highly recommend using the option "manual CPC." There are two other options, but before we delve into those, I'd like to take some time to explain how you can structure your ads via ad sets and campaigns. Those of you who have experience with this can safely skip down to the section on bidding.

The uppermost level of your ads is called a campaign. For example, if you're selling a particular cocktail party dress for women, you can label your campaign as "cocktail party dress ad campaign." Below the campaign level comes the ad set. An ad set is usually setup to indicate or compare one demographic with another.

For example, one possible ad set could be "cocktail party dress 18-30," which indicates that the ads within this campaign are targeting women between the ages of 18 to 30. Another ad set could target those between the ages of 30-45. Another for those over 45 and so on. It's not just about age. You could split your audience based on other factors too.

One ad set could target women who earn more than $100,000 per year, regardless of age, another above $150,000, another above $50,000 and so on. Below the ad set level is the actual ad itself. You can have as many ads as you want and experience advertisers usually run what are called A/B tests between versions of ads. I'll talk about these in a later chapter, but for now, understand that there is no limit to the number of ads you can setup or ad sets and campaigns for that matter.

Now, with all that out of the way, let's look at bidding methods.

Bids

I've already mentioned manual CPC. This option allows you to manually set the bid and fix the bid to a particular price. Google will not adjust the bid amount, and you will thus have complete control over your budget. If your budget is less, then go for this option. Even if you have a large budget and are doing this for the first time, use this. The other option you have is automatic CPC.

This option is aimed at those people who manage a large number of ads, and it reduces the time they need to spend monitoring and adjusting bids on each individual ad. For bigger brands, this can save hours upon hours of time since they'll probably have hundreds of ads running at once.

So how does this work exactly? Well, Google will monitor your ads' performance and if your ads start receiving negative performance such as losing impressions thanks to new competitors coming in, it will raise your bid to make sure you remain competitive. The downside of this is that you cannot set a max CPC since Google might need to adjust it higher than that amount.

Therefore, you pay for the convenience by sacrificing some control over your budget. This is not as alarming as it sounds, and it isn't as if you're going to end up with a huge bill the moment you do this. Google is quite smart adjusting your bids and has a number of options that you can choose to optimize your ads and make your spend more efficient.

The bidding options Google gives you are:

1. Target CPA

2. Target ROAS (Return on ad spend)

3. Maximize conversions

4. Enhanced CPC

5. Maximize clicks

6. Manual CPC (we looked at this already)

7. Target search page location

8. Target outranking share

9. CPM bidding

10. CPM bidding

11. CPV bidding

12. Target impression share bidding

This is a lot! Don't worry, though, you don't need to master all of these at once. Instead, simply use the most popular ones and you'll be just fine. The first popular automated strategy is enhanced CPC, #4 on the list above.

ECPC allows Google to smartly adjust your bid based on the competition. For example, if the top spot is easily attainable by increasing the bid just a little bit, Google will do it. However, if the spots are facing high competition, it'll lower your bid since you'll have lesser chances of converting. Google will usually average out the costs to stay in line with your target maximum spend and bids so that you don't spend too much per click.

Maximizing conversions is another simple and popular strategy. Google will simply ensure that it shows your ads to people who are the most likely to convert on your website. In other words, those who will pay you money. Bids will be automatically raised or lowered and are limited to the maximum budget per day.

A popular bidding strategy to utilize if you wish to increase brand awareness is the CPM bidding strategy. Here you'll be paying for impressions and such campaigns are not well suited for search result campaigns but for display network ones. What's the difference, you might be wondering? Well, let's look at this.

Networks

When you setup your ads on Google, you will have to choose which networks your ads show up in. The first and most obvious option is the search network. These refer to ads that show up on top of search results on Google's first page. Next, we have the display network.

This refers to banner ads on blogs and websites that have installed AdSense. If you're unaware of what this is, AdSense is a blog monetization tool where Google pays blog owners money to display ads on their websites. With such ads, you will be paying per impression mostly and your ads will be matched with the niche the website or blog is in. As you can imagine, keyword targeting doesn't really apply here and therefore, it is hard to optimize for sales.

Generally, display network campaigns work best for those looking to increase brand awareness and increase their visibility. Next up we have the shopping ad campaign, which will result in your product being shown as a listing when people search for a particular keyword. Those in ecommerce often use this quite effectively.

A video campaign is another option Google gives you, and this involves integration with YouTube. I'll talk about this in detail in a later chapter. There are many ad formats you can run, and despite the bad press YouTube ads receive generally, they do provide great ROI for advertisers.

Lastly, you can set up an app campaign if you're releasing an app. Google will create the ad for you by taking data from your app from the Play store and design the most optimized version of it. For purposes of this book, this sort of campaign doesn't really apply, so I'm not going to address it too much.

With PPC ads, you'll be looking mostly at search or display network ads, so let's look at how you can optimize these further.

Bid Modifiers

There are ways to optimize your bids and these are called geographic, dayparting, and device optimization. What this means is that depending on certain qualities within these three criteria, you can increase or decrease your bids amounts for a better ROI.

Geographic refers to where a person is accessing Google from. For example, if you're selling surfboard, someone in California is more likely to use one than someone in North Dakota. You can elect to bid more for the person in California. Similarly, user behavior is different depending on the device they're using.

Someone who searches for stuff on their desktop is more likely to buy your product than on mobile. Therefore, you can optimize for purchases made via desktop and instead run brand awareness campaigns on mobile and so on. Depending on your product, you could even choose to completely exclude certain devices.

Lastly, we have dayparting that allows you to control your bids on the basis of the days of the week. If you're running ads to generate sales leads for a law firm, you're more likely to be receiving relevant clicks during weekdays than during weekends. Depending on your product, you want to optimize your ads based on when your customer is most likely to be searching for it.

That brings us to the end of AdWords basics. It's a lot of information, especially is you've never run PPC campaigns before. However, with baby steps you'll find that a lot of it makes sense and it really isn't that difficult to get your head around.

Chapter 2: Keyword Research

The entire internet runs on keywords. While keywords are not a perfect approximation of what we're really searching for, it is the best thing currently available and all of Google is centered around how keywords work and how to dissect them for better relevance with regard to displaying search results.

Get your keywords right, and you'll ensure that your campaigns will turn you a profit. Remember that your keywords need to be relevant as well to have your ads displayed in good positions. There's also the competition to worry about, as in how much are your competitors bidding and what are they bidding on.

So let's take a look at all of this.

Keyword Initial Preparation

Often, people will rush into a keyword planning tool and being to generate keywords without giving a thought to how they're paid ad campaigns tie in with the rest of their business aims. The fact is that your advertising campaigns are just a part of your overall content strategy, and you should know this inside and out before you begin.

Truth be told, I could write an entire book on content strategy so I'm not going to go too deeply into it on here. However, you should have the basics of your content strategy covered. For example, you should know who your customer is, which stage of growth you're currently in, and the steps of your sales funnel.

Your sales funnel is integral to the success of your ad campaigns since you will have different keywords for different levels of it. For example, someone who is searching for "red cocktail dress best price" is further along the buying cycle than someone who searches for "red cocktail dress." Your content strategy is where you will also receive your first keywords.

Brainstorm

You will be targeting some keywords as part of your SEO efforts, so begin with these. These are quite a powerful bunch because if you manage to dominate the paid ads, odds are that Google will reward you in the organic rankings as well. Generally speaking, there are four categories of keywords you want to brainstorm:

1. Brand

2. Related

3. Competitor

4. Generic

A brand keyword relates to your particular brand as is obvious by the name. An example of this "Caroline Herrera red cocktail dress." Generic keywords are those that generally describe your product or service. For example "cocktail dress red" or "cocktail dress for women" are generic keywords.

Related keywords are those which complement your product. "Jewelry for women," "shoes for women," etc. are examples of stuff that people will buy along with your main product. A good way to brainstorm good ideas for these is to head over to Amazon.com (the Google of shopping) to look up a product similar to yours.

Under the product listing is a section that says "people who bought this item also bought." Make a list of the stuff in there and take note of any brand names that popup during your research. Finally, we have competitor keywords. These are brand keywords containing your competitors' names in them.

Make a list of all of them, and classify them accordingly. Do the same in terms of classifying them according to where they rank in your sales funnel. Next, add additional action terms to them, which indicate intent. Examples include words like "best" or "comparison," "best deal," "discount," and so on. Remember to add misspellings on your product's name or of your brand as well.

Once your preliminary list is created and classified, head over to the Google keyword planner (GKP) tool.

Refine

The GKP has received a lot of flak for the way Google has structured it. It used to be completely free, but now Google has decided that it might as well make some money off of it and forces you to spend money on a campaign to access exact search volume data. In fact, they even go to extreme lengths to try to trick you into believing that the tool itself is only accessible if you run an AdWords campaign.

Let me make one thing clear: the biggest difference between the paid and free version is that the paid version will give you exact search volume data for a keyword. That's it. You can use the keyword tool for free. All you need to do is to indicate to Google that you're experienced with Google Ads. This is usually a little link at the bottom of the initial AdWords Express page that Google shows you when you go into AdWords.

If you're unclear as to how this works, head over the Ahrefs blog (Patel, 2017) and search for how you can access the tool for free. Their guide has great graphics and shows you how to do this step by step. Anyway, back to the tool. Once you have access, plug in a few keywords into the keywords box separated by commas. Choose your appropriate product category as well.

Next, set your targeting and language correctly. If you're targeting worldwide customers, unless the product happens to be something super specific, simply choose United States since search volumes are the highest from here. Choose the "Google" option under the network to exclude the display network and click "get ideas."

Make sure you're searching for broad matches since this gives you the most ideas. You'll find this filtering on the right hand column. Once your results show, you'll see the exact search volume if you've spent some money on AdWords already. If not, you'll see a range. This is a bit annoying but, either way, the ranges are correct. The third column will show you the average CPC for each keyword. The column is labeled "suggested bid."

The column in between the CPC and the keyword name is titled "competition" and this refers to the number of advertisers who are bidding for that keyword. Now, here's what you need to do next. Take your list of keywords and look at the ones that are branded or are generic. Stick to the high level ones and not keywords that are very specific. You can keep these, but don't worry about them now.

The point is to use these high level keywords as seed keywords, and let Google give you more ideas on how to take it forward from there.

How to Find the Best Keywords

Starting from the first, plug in your seed keyword into the keyword research tool and look at what Google gives you as suggestions. Google is going to give you a bunch of stuff so take the time to look through these keywords to see if any of them spark interest in you or sound like something your potential buyer will search for.

Remember to keep the idea of the sales funnel in mind. You want to target customers who are in the final stages of the buying process since they are the most likely to pay you money. For example, if your seed keyword is "women's cocktail party dress" and one of the suggestions is "cocktail dress styles," this is not a buyer keyword. It indicates that person searching for this is looking for information and is doing her research.

Remember you're paying per click so you want to maximize your opportunities. You will face higher competition but with a high quality ad, you can have extremely profitable campaigns so don't worry about this. Go through at least four pages of the results you get in the tool and add them to your keyword plan, which is an option at the top.

Export these to a spreadsheet and then repeat the process again until you're done with all of your seed keywords. As you keep moving down your seed keywords list, you'll find that Google will keep suggesting stuff you've already noted down. This is not a problem and is to be expected since you're obviously searching for related terms.

A word of caution here: don't shy away from including keywords that have low search volume. Often, people come at this with an SEO mindset where you want to avoid the low search volume keywords. However, with paid ads, low volume simply means cheaper clicks so don't discard these. Repeat the process with your branded keywords as well, and by the end of this you'll have a large spreadsheet full of ideas. Now, it's time to get to work on these.

Refine Further

As you review your ds, you'll notice that some of them belong in categories together. Create columns of categories, or different sheets if need be, and group these similar keywords together. Each of these categories can be a separate campaign or ad set for you to run later on. While doing this, you'll find that you'll have some keywords that aren't particularly high in terms of buyer's intention. No matter, simply categorize them as content marketing keywords and use them for SEO.

Now, from this large list of keywords you have it's time to decide on which ones to advertise on. This is a subjective decision, and you will need to make some guesses here. Your ultimate goal for a visitor to your page also plays an important part. If you're advertising for brand awareness, you might want to include search terms that are further up in the funnel than ones that are below and so on.

Deciding whether the keyword conforms to your product is also a good filter to use. As much as possible, it helps to be specific. This means if someone is searching for a "garden dress," don't advertise your cocktail dress for it. The quality score metric will ensure that your ad will not deliver a great ROI, no matter how high your margins might be.

Keep an eye out for negative keywords. These are keywords you DON'T want your potential buyers to be searching. For example, if you're sick of bargain hunters like everyone else in the retail industry is, terms such as "best discount red cocktail dress" and so on is a negative keyword. This excludes people you don't want anything to do with when it comes to your product.

Sometimes, your related keywords that you will have pulled from Google will have negative keywords within them. Remember to classify them as a separate category so you can set these up within your campaigns.

Now that you have your list of keywords, it's time to take the next step and develop the structure of your campaigns.

Structure

So how should you split these keywords into campaigns and ad sets? On a high level you should have separate campaigns for your brand name, your competitors' brand names, and for different languages and countries if your product has global appeal or if you're targeting worldwide markets.

Next, the ad set level should be differentiated on the basis of intent as well as product type. In our example you're advertising just a single dress so this shouldn't be an issue. However, if you're also selling shoes, then obviously this goes into a different ad set. Remember that these ad sets will also break down similarly in your other campaigns. some advertisers get pretty extreme with their ad sets, choosing a single keyword within each.

This is a bit much in my opinion, but there's no denying that you should keep your ad sets as small as possible. How small depends on your comfort level when it comes to managing the campaign. Keep in mind that it's a lot easier to track keyword performance at the ad set level if you've grouped them tightly.

Loosely grouping your keywords will mean you will need to always dive down to the keyword level to monitor your stats and this simply takes time. Ideally, you can take one look at your ad sets and get a firm grasp on how the keywords in there are doing. Once all of this is done, you're officially ready to go live!

Paid Tools

The GKP is free to use and if you're short on budget, I'd suggest sticking to just this. However, if you've got the money to invest then you should consider investing in a paid tool like Moz and Ahrefs. Despite the annoying names, these products are actually excellent and will give you an additional edge when it comes to identifying great keywords ("How To Do Keyword Research For Google Ads", 2019).

Moz's keyword explorer will actually give you suggestions from your seed keywords, and this will save you a lot of time during the brainstorming portion of keyword research. Not only this it will give you the relevance of each term along with the respective search volume as well. This is pretty useful for SEO too as you can imagine.

Another paid tool you can use is SEMrush, which actually helps you spy on your competitors directly. Once you search for a particular keyword, you can see who is advertising for it and also what their ad copy looks like. In addition, you will also receive a list of suggested keywords that will closely match the other keywords they're bidding on. Invaluable stuff!

If you're really uptight about getting the most exact search volume data, you can choose to invest in Ahrefs. This does pretty much the same things as SEMrush and Moz, except for the competitor spying part, which you'll need to work around. Either way, you can't go wrong with any of these tools. While they are not designed for paid ads specifically, they will help your business' SEO and content outreach efforts.

A lot of the time, you don't need to go outside for great keyword ideas. If your website has been up and running for a while, you can simply look at Google Analytics and analyze the organic search data and the site search to check out what people are looking for. This is not of much use to a beginner, but it is a valuable source of keywords nonetheless.

You can try to analyze Google Trends to check out what is trending and whether any of your seed keyword ideas, or other ones for that matter, are declining in popularity. Google Alerts is another great tool that you can use for SEO and backlinking but keeps you up to date with what's going on in your niche. This is not a keyword tool per se but more of a topic alert and can give you ideas as to which direction things are headed in.

As you can hopefully see by now, keyword research for your paid campaigns tie in strongly with your overall content strategy. In fact, a lot of your keywords will simply be offshoots or a subset of your main keyword research efforts for SEO. So cast a wide net for keywords and categorize them carefully.

Oh, and also consider their match types.

Match Types

I'd mentioned previously that Google gives you three match types when it comes to keywords. Understanding how these work will often make a huge difference in your campaigns. Here they are:

1. Broad

2. Phrase

3. Exact

Broad matches mean that Google will consider all combinations of your keyword. For example, if your keyword is "red cocktail dress," it will include the following keywords as broad matches:

- Red cocktail dress for women

- Big red cocktail dress for summer for women

- Cocktail dress for women red color

- Discount cocktail dress for women red

and so on.

There are innumerable possibilities when it comes to expanding this list since a broad match implies that any word within the keyword can be considered a valid match. As you can imagine, this leads to generating matches for a bunch of keywords that might have nothing to do with your product. This is where the phrase match comes in.

The phrase match keeps the exact phrasing of your keyword when it comes to matching it to appropriate searches. So the order of the words in "red cocktail dress" will remain the same and will not be switched around. This reduces the overall number of keywords greatly, but your targeting will be more focused.

This doesn't mean to say that broad matches are bad and phrase matches are good. For some keywords, broad matches might give you a better return. This is especially true for long tail keywords. Long tail keywords contain three or more words and are very specific searches users enter. "Red cocktail dress for women size 5" is a very specific search.

The color is specified, the style of the dress is named clearly, and the size is mentioned as well. If this customer were to walk into your store and ask for this you would not show them a pair of jeans. People who search in this hyper specific manner are great for businesses. The problem from an ads standpoint with this keyword is that it limits your world greatly. What if they're very keen on the size being a 5 but are open to a green dress as well?

Hence, a broad match with a long tail keyword gives you more options while still managing to be specific. Google will still bring up cocktail dresses but will play around with the size and the color just a little bit. It isn't doing this consciously, but the results play out this way because the keyword is very specific to begin with. A broad match simply loosens the reins a bit.

With high level keywords, you want to go the other way and specify a phrase match or an exact match, which is the third type of match. As the name suggests, Google will use the exact phrasing of the keyword when matching it with searches. If your high level keyword is "dresses for women." Google is not going to bring your ad up when someone searches for "jeans for women."

As tempting as the exact match is, you should use it only if you've done the research and have data to validate that a particular keyword is exactly what people search for. Often branded keywords or keywords that specifically associate themselves with your brand are good bets for exact matches. During initial stages of your campaign, you want to stick to the first two types. As you gather more data, you can play around with exact matches to see if they work. If it doesn't, you can always revert back to what worked originally.

The Next Step

Once your keywords are up and running as part of a campaign (I'll show you how to set one up in a later chapter), you will need to monitor performance. Here's the thing: ads take time to receive clicks, and you will need to be patient. Everyone wants results yesterday, but it just doesn't work like this.

At a minimum, you should give your ads a week or around twenty clicks to pass judgment on it. Without that, you're making choices based on thin air. So give your ads some time and keep monitoring their performance. From a keyword research standpoint, you will receive even more suggestions as your data comes in.

For one, you'll be able to see which keywords don't perform and you can add these to your negative keyword list. Next, within the "search terms" report, which is under a tab of the same name, you'll be able to view additional suggestions and monitor existing keyword performance. If you've missed some keywords from back when you were flipping through multiple pages of the keyword tool, here's where you get your chance to add more of them to your campaigns.

As you receive more clicks, it becomes a matter of optimization. Keep your ROI in mind as you enable or disable your keywords. This isn't a set and forget process, so you need to be active. Having said that, you don't need to be glued to the screen at all times. Google gives you a mountain of data and options, but take your time understanding all of it and expand your knowledge slowly and steadily.

A crucial part of business is figuring out where you stand vis-a-vis your competitors. Let's look at how to do this next.

Chapter 3: Competitor Research

There is a possibility of you going down the rabbit hole from which you may never emerge when it comes to analyzing your competitors. It's easy to get carried away and nitpick every single thing your competitors are doing and seeing how you can beat them. When this starts happening, you've unconsciously shifted your goal from making profits to beating your competitors.

However, you can't ignore the competition as well. It's sad to say this, but if you don't keep tabs on your competition, you'll find that they'll sneak up on you and in some industries underhanded tactics are the norm, such as clicking on competitors ads repeatedly to drive up costs and the feared branded keyword bidding war.

In this chapter, I'll give you a method to spy on what your competition is up to as well as give you methods that will help you take advantage of their weaknesses in a safe and inexpensive way. Before all of this, though, remember that you're in business to make money, not beat the daylights out of your competition. You can achieve the #1 spot across all keywords, but the costs involved might not make this worth it. Even worse, you could play into your competitor's hands by doing that.

So, always keep things in perspective and keep your ego out of it.

Competitor Insight

You should have a rough idea of who your competitors are as part of the niche research process when you first setup your online business or outlet. So figuring out who they are should not be much of a problem. If you don't know who your competition is because you simply don't care, well, you do need to care because in the online world, the competition can push your margins over the edge if you don't keep tabs on them.

Competitor insight is a tactic that a lot of bigger companies use and doing it all by yourself is going to take some time. If you're a one person shop, then you need to evaluate the reward versus the time investment. If you can spend that time making more money then I'd say you're better off doing that. Competitor analysis is all about reducing your costs, as opposed to making money so making this your primary focus is not wise.

Furthermore, the best tools to analyze the competition happen to be paid so it's not as if you can do this for free. Considering the investment you've made in your business or personal brand, you should not hesitate to invest in a competitor analysis tool since such tools can help you out with SEO as well.

There is a free option, but this doesn't give you much insight. The free option is the GKP, which is downright clunky and sometimes actively unhelpful in comparison to the competition. So keep all of this in mind as you go through this chapter.

Auctions

The standard format for determining listing position in online ads is an auction. This suits the ad networks perfectly because it tends to drive up prices beyond what they ought to be. Think back to a time when you went to an auction. Odds are that the environment itself caused you to bid above your planned budget and you probably ended up with a roll of toilet paper signed by some ball player who was once famous.

My point is that, auction environments tend to screw with the wiring in our brains and get us giddy. Meanwhile, the ad networks sit there and watch everyone scrambling to outbid one another. This auction system actively works against advertisers, and no number of Q scores is ever going to fix this. Still, this is the world you're dealing with so you might as well accept it.

I'm mentioning all of this as a prelude to the concept of bidding on branded keywords. We've looked at what these are already and once your campaigns are running, you'll notice that your own brand's keywords will be dirt cheap in terms of CPC metrics. The reason for this is because your relevancy and Q score is off the charts for your own brand and understandably so. Once you begin to get results from your brand name, a curious thing will happen.

You'll find that your competitors will begin to show up in the ad spots below you, and in some cases, they'll even outrank you if the keyword is tangentially brand related. Why is this happening? Well, remember how you plugged in your competitors' brand names as keywords in the previous chapter? This is what they're doing to you. At this point, you have a choice to make.

Do you want to engage in a bidding war over brand names or not? Getting into a bidding war is worth it because if you don't respond in some way, your CPC for your own brand name is going to escalate, which is a ridiculous situation to be in. After all, it's your brand so it should be the cheapest for you to bid on. Your ROI also gets messed up as costs go higher.

However, engage too much with your competition and you'll realize that not only are costs rising astronomically, both of you are increasing each other's costs and that neither of you stands a chance of making any money if such a state of affairs continues. Sometimes, you'll run into competitors who simply want to burn everything and in such cases, your only option is to minimize your losses.

So before dealing with how to increase your upside through competitor analysis, I'd like to take some time to look at how to cover your downside first. You will be engaged in a bidding war at some point, so it's best to be prepared before this happens.

Downside Cover

The most effective strategy and the one that you should perform as default is to trademark your brand name. This will stop people from poaching your brand name and using it in their ads. For example, if you're an up and coming shoe seller, but don't trademark your brand, there is nothing stopping Nike or Adidas from explicitly calling you out in their ads by saying "much better than average Joe's shoes!"

Upstanding companies usually won't do this, but the internet has its share of scumbags so you need to protect your brand from begin hijacked like this. Besides it protects you from false claims and slander. Applying for a brand trademark is straightforward and there are easily available, free guides online. If you haven't done this as yet, go ahead and get started right now.

Once your trademark is approved, you can monitor Google for mentions of your brand and report violations to them. Google has very strict policies against trademark violation, and they take it quite seriously. So always be on the lookout for your own brand's mentions, whether they're positive or negative.

One of the natural conclusions from all of this is that you cannot mention your competitor's brand name in your ads directly. In some cases, you can use names in a certain context. This often applies to brand names that also happen to be common words. A good example is Budget Car Rental. The word budget can be used in some contexts, but the hassle of dealing with trademark violation notices and resolving them might not be worth the time for you.

While trademarking is a strategy you can execute physically, the next one is more of a mental thing. Understand the downsides of getting into a bidding war and check to see if your competitor is bidding on your brand. Often a gentleman's agreement exists between competitors in certain niches and if your competition is not targeting your brand names, don't target theirs.

Targeting their brand in an unprovoked manner is a red flag and unless you're prepared to handle the negative fallout from that, don't do it. Negative fallouts aside from hugely increased costs include a poor brand image for the both of you. The customer might not know what's going on behind the scenes but the message often comes across in subliminal ways and ultimately, you'll find that no one wins.

My point is, avoid a bidding war right up until you absolutely cannot. Do not ever go looking for one. Now, let's look at what you can do to spy on your competitors and avoid a bidding war.

Getting Started

The easiest way to obtain insight into your competitors is to head over to the GKP and pull up the auction insights report. This report, like everything with Google Ads, will have a ton of data and it's easy to get lost in all of it. Here's what you need to pay special attention to:

- Impression share

- Overlap rate

- Position above rate

- Top of page rate

- Outranking share

Impression share can be a bit confusing, so let's look at this first. You will see your own data in all of these columns in the report, but since you're looking at your competitors, your focus need not be on this. Your impression share number is the percentage of the number of times your ad was shown divided by the number of times your ad was eligible to be shown.

In other words, how many times did you lineup to be picked to play and how many times were you picked. If this number is low, you might want to look at boosting your Q score a touch. Anyway, my point is that the number for your competitors are not calculated the same way. Instead, your competitors' impression share is how often their ads showed up in auctions you were also involved in. Using the previous example, of all the times the both of you were vying for a spot in the team how often were they picked? If their impression share is far higher than yours, they're probably being picked more often and in favor of you.

Comparing both numbers is not a like for like thing, so don't read too much into this. Just be aware of significant differences between both. If huge differences exist, then it's a sign that your ads aren't performing as well compared to theirs.

The overlap rate makes comparison a bit easier. This is the number of times your competitor's ad received an impression when your ad was shown as well. This number is expressed as a percentage. So 77% indicates that their ad was shown along with yours 77% of the time for that keyword.

The next metric is the positive above rate and this indicates how many times your competitor's ads were shown above yours in auctions where both of your ads received impressions. The top of the page rate indicates how often your ads and your competitors were shown above the search results when people searched for that keyword.

Lastly, we have the outranking share that is a measure of how often your ad showed up higher in the results than your competitors ad. Remember to look at your own row to get a feel for this since the other rows will show how many times the other auction participants' ads showed higher than yours.

When combined together, you'll get a fair view of how well your ad is performing compared to the competition. Next, it's time to categorize them.

Categorization

Your competition will come in different flavors but the most common ones will be the following:

1. Affiliates

2. Marketing partners

3. Resellers

4. Frauds

5. Aggregators

6. True competitors

Let's deal with the most problematic one right off the bat. The frauds are the ones who are simply using your brand name to push their own services and such people are more prevalent than you might first think. This is why trademarking your brand is so important. Please note that trademarking only prevents them from mentioning your brand name in their ads. It won't stop them from targeting your brand name as a keyword.

Aggregators are simply comparison shopping sites, which will pull together prices from across a number of places and show them in one place. As such, these aren't a problem since if your product is good enough, the traffic will be redirected to you anyway. With regard to affiliates and marketing partners, it is important to have clear discussions about which keywords they cannot be bidding on and which ones you will stay out of.

This helps all of you keep CPC costs down and prevents you from inflating each other's costs by mistake. As for your true competitors, it's time to dig deeper into them.

Areas of Competition

Which keywords are the ones which are experiencing the highest degree of competition? This is the place for you to start when you dig deeper into your competition. This is easier said than done if you have multiple product lines. A good idea is to simply group together all of your keywords into categories and to monitor them in this manner.

You can use third party paid tools to do this or simply head over to the dimensions tab in the Google Ads dashboard and you can create a pivot table, like in Excel, to group the keywords that are performing the best. Monitor the performance of these keywords and setup alerts with regard to their performance.

This will help you react quickly to changes in your best keywords and stay ahead of the competition. Next, you need to monitor your competitors' messaging and ad copy. The best way, and only way aside from repeatedly searching for keywords on Google manually, is to use a paid tool. I'll talk about using these in more detail in the next section.

Once you've been monitoring your competitors' ad copy for a while and if you're noticing their ads seem to be performing better than yours, you can tweak your ad copy for better results. A good idea is to A/B test this to see what works best, which you'll learn later in this book.

Using Paid Tools

Now that you have a good handle on which keywords are performing the best for you and which ones you're lagging behind your competitors in, it's time to dive into the paid tools to dissect the opposition further. The first tool we'll look at is SpyFu. The interface is pretty simple to use and while the data isn't fully accurate, it is close enough to be meaningful.

Enter the keyword you and your competitors are bidding over and the tool will give you the CTR, the number of other advertisers bidding on that keyword as well as other keyword suggestions. This data is pretty helpful for those who decided to skip Google's data and head over there directly. Also, in terms of keyword research, this data is invaluable.

The really good stuff is over in the "advertiser history" section, where you can see a full calendar history of ads your competition has been running. You'll be able to see how their copy has changed and get a good grip on what they're trying to achieve with their ads. Using all of this you can judge whether your own ad copy needs tweaking or not.

SEMRush also offers a similar tool, although they don't explicitly list the number of competitors. Instead, you'll receive the expected CPC and a score that indicates the level of competition along with a list of who they are. Well, all of this is pretty vanilla, you might be thinking, since Google gives you this for free.

However, the best part of SEMRush is that you can click on the competitor and actually unearth the keywords they're bidding on along with the amount they're spending on their bids (Patel,

2017). Not only that you'll also receive an estimated CPC. From experience, this number isn't fully accurate but it is close enough.

So between Google's data and one of these paid tools, you can pretty much recreate your competitor's entire ad campaign. Recreating all of it is one thing, but how do you now take advantage of this data? We've already seen how going after brand names is a bad idea and will place you in a war you can't win, even if you emerge on top. So what are the best ways of targeting your competition without shooting yourself in the foot?

Better Discounts

When shopping on the internet, the biggest pain point is the price. People are looking for the best deal. Therefore, use this to your advantage by slashing your prices as low as you can go. Perhaps you can improve your offer by giving your customers some additional service for free.

Since you have the competition's ad copy in front of you, you'll know what number to target. Offering a better price than your competition is a pretty easy way to stand out. By doing this you can target their brand keywords without explicitly using their trademarks in your ad.

Even if you cannot go much lower than where you are, consider offering introductory or one off offers. This will bring more customers into your funnel, and once they're there you can upsell them on another service or product. This is a common tactic that big sellers use. If you are going to do this, make sure you map your workflow out in advance so you know exactly what your acquisition costs need to be well in advance

Better Value

While price is one thing, value is entirely another. Can you offer something that your competitor cannot do? Is there some feature of your product or service that addresses a particular pain point? Brainstorm how your product is better than the rest and sell this idea when targeting your competitor.

A risky but profitable strategy is to use your competitor's name in your ad and differentiate yourself. This works very well if your competitor is a huge business and you're operating in a very small niche in that business. In such cases, you can often get away with using their brand name in your headline since you're not negatively mentioning them but simply claiming a likeness within a focused niche.

It's a good idea to verify whether you can actually do this before putting it into action. There are a few loopholes you can exploit, but Google enforces each one a bit differently so make sure to check this out in advance.

Better Extensions

Google allows you to use a bunch of extensions within your ads, and your choices here will impact how well your ads are received. Analyze your competition to see if there's something you can improve on. One popular extension to use is social proof. If your product has received ratings, you can display this within your ad to convince people to click.

Doing this is really about finding gaps in your competition and then exploiting that. Can you highlight your product better? Can you use extensions to call out specific audiences who might be interested in your product? This applies especially to those in the internet marketing software niche or SEO tools niche.

Above all else, remember that the point is to drive traffic to yourself first and foremost. Only once this is done should you turn your attention to siphoning traffic away from your competition. Avoid bidding wars like the plague and minimize the damage as much as possible if you find yourself in one.

So we've looked at keywords and also now looked at what the competition is doing. You're all set right? Well, not quite. It's time to consider what happens when the user clicks your ad.

Chapter 4: Landing Page Design

Imagine taking out a full page ad in the New York Times convincing people to buy your amazing product, which is located conveniently close to them at one of your locations. Now imagine backing up this ad with a storefront that is dirty, badly lit, and staffed by your surly uncle Bob.

As ridiculous as this sounds, this is precisely what people on the internet do. They go through all the trouble of creating ad campaigns and spending all that money on driving people to their website and once people get there, they just forget about all of it and negate their good work by designing a terrible landing page.

You've already learned that your landing page design affects your quality score. Google monitors this via the bounce rate of visitors to your site. You might have the best product or the best service but if your page isn't designed right, no one is going to buy anything from you.

Even worse, it'll start costing you more to bring people on board with your product.

Steps to Conversions

Your landing page refers to the webpage your prospective customers will land one once they click your ad. This can be a standalone page or a product display page. Either choice can work depending on the product and the offer. For limited, one time offers you should try a single page while for products and services that you offer regularly, a page within your website is a good idea.

The landing page is your biggest asset when it comes to achieving profitability so ensuring optimal design will pay huge dividends. If designing a page seems too intimidating, consider hiring a professional to do this for you. With that being said, there are some simple steps you can follow to achieve success.

Research

This is obvious, but you should know your customer pretty well before you design your page. The best way to create an efficient landing page is to know your customers' motivation and to simply give them exactly what it is they're looking for. Easier said than done!

The good news is that market research doesn't have to cost too much these days thanks to the internet. Your first step should be to head over to Google Trends to see if your niche and related topics are still relevant or facing any headwinds. Assuming this looks good, you can proceed to the next step.

Just a note at this point: you can use these exact steps to research a niche as well. If you feel confident you know your niche and your customer pretty well, feel free to skip to the next section since I'll be talking exclusively about research in this portion.

The next step is to get into the mindset of your shopper. Generally speaking, women tend to be easier to figure out when it comes to shopping patterns than men. This is simply because there's more data on women shopping as compared to men (Patel, 2017). Men also tend to break a few of the patterns one expects from shoppers so if your product is aimed at men, this step is doubly important for you.

Here are the steps any shopper or user looking for your service/product goes through:

1. Awareness of the problem- "I need xxx"

2. Research- "Where/how/why/when can I get xxx"

3. Ready to Buy- "Which is the best place to buy xxx"

4. Buy- "I've bought xxx"

5. Post buy- "How did that feel?"

Your landing page is going to be concerned with items one through four. The post purchase process involves keeping them updated of offers and products via email and remarketing efforts. Designing a simple landing page that will address all the four points is not an easy task and requires further exploration.

A good place to conduct research to get to know the problem better is social media. If you don't have existing channels, join groups that are dedicated to the topic and get a feel for what people are going through. Facebook, Twitter, and forums are the best places to conduct this research. For some products, especially information related ones, Reddit is a gold mine of customer pain since the nature of that website is for people to be unfiltered.

You can even pitch your product to people within these groups with a view to testing demand prior to release. Just be careful to have built up some equity with the group before doing so. A key thing to remember at this point is that people often say they want something solved but really want something else.

This often drives marketers mad, as you can imagine. There's no template to figure this out, unfortunately, but you'll have to feel your way through it. A good example of this is if people have a problem and say they want coaching on getting past it, what they really want is one on one sessions and mentoring of some kind (Patel, 2017).

The final step in your research process is to figure out the intent behind the keywords you're using to target your customers. What are they really looking for? Are they being specific about something or not? Placing keywords within your sales funnel is a good way to get a handle on this.

Now that you know you visitor through and through, it's time to design the page.

Design

While the copy on your page is the most important driver of conversions, your design determines a large part of whether your visitors will even read your copy in the first place (Patel, 2017). It's easy to dismiss design as something that needs to be "clean" and "functional," whatever the hell those words mean.

The best way to get started is to use a simple template. This is, in fact, the same process I advocate for writing copy as well since in the beginning, there's no need to reinvent the wheel. People have found tried and tested methods that work so simply reuse those templates for your purposes.

The first item in the landing page template is the headline that is relevant to the keyword that was clicked by your visitor along with a sub header that provides supplementary information. Next, you need to have a video or an eye catching image of some kind on the left hand side of your page. This will be the upper left hand side of your page when viewed as a whole.

Why is this? Well, research shows that people online like to read in an F-shaped pattern with their eyes settling to the left, going down and then moving to the upper right side and skipping lines as they move down the page (Patel, 2017). The upper left image or hero shot as it's known, captures their attention. On the opposite side of the hero shot is the form where people enter their information to sign up for your offer or to buy you product.

It might seem a bit too early to introduce a buy button so high up on the page, but this is for customers who have already done their research. Often, you'll find that after checking out your landing page "one," people will visit it repeatedly to do more research and then finally click that link on top because there's no point scrolling down anymore.

A single scroll down or half scroll down, below the hero shot, is where social proof is posted. Social proof can be a testimonial of your product or service or it could be a simple rating. Below all of this is where your copy really begins. At this point, you will introduce your product and pitch your proposition to the visitor.

Here is where you need to follow a standard copywriting template, which I'll talk about in the next section. It is also a good idea to include a few more testimonials as social proof of the fact that your product works. Up to this point, if your reader is still on your page, you have succeeded in hooking them in. Now, it's time to go deeper.

You will introduce the next section of your page by providing a hook or reinforcement statement that keeps them reading and showcase at least four or five benefits they will receive by using your product. At the end of this section is another Call to Action or CTA where you'll prompt them to buy your product.

If your product happens to be technical, it is a good idea to replicate the previous section all over again since you will need to fully explain technical details to those who cannot fully understand it. This is why you will find landing pages for some software products tend to go on and on.

You may have noticed that this structure has elements that are applicable only to a single landing page. What if you have an e-Commerce store and are linking your ads directly to your product page? Well, the same principles apply here as well. In place of your hero shot, you will need to have a high quality image of your product.

The description of the product goes on the left along with the price. Place a CTA either below the description or to the right hand side of it if your website template can accommodate three columns. Below this, you can showcase reviews. A good idea is to simply copy the template that Amazon uses. They're the biggest shopping site in the world, so if it works for them it should work for you.

Getting back to our single landing page case, how long should it be? Let's look at this and some other design elements now.

Length and Other Considerations

I'll make this easy for you: the greater the level of commitment your product requires you customer to offer, the longer your landing page should be. If you're selling something that's not very expensive or part of your customer demographic, you need not bother with long copy and this will simply be a waste of time.

Think of it as you walking into a place to buy an expensive product. If you know nothing about it, it is unlikely you'll buy something the first time you walk in. You'll spend time doing research and getting the know the sales staff (assuming it isn't available online) and only on your fourth or fifth visit will you shell out the cash to buy it. That pack of gum by the grocery checkout aisle, though? You don't think twice before adding that to your shopping.

So think of your landing pages the same way. This is the final step of your funnel and people are prescreened thanks to the keyword you have used to lure them here, but you still need to respect the level of commitment you're asking of them. A good tip is to keep the design simple and clean.

Using high quality images and videos are a great way to do this. Depending on your niche and offer, an image might be better than a video. If you're pitching your services as an SEO expert, you're better off pasting a high quality image of yourself or your results in the hero shot.

If you're selling something related to personal development, a video might work better. A lot of landing page designer software will give you the chance to a/b test your pages so take advantage of this fully. What's more, you can even choose to customize your page so that it shows a bit differently for different keywords.

Previously, you had to create different landing pages for every single ad set you had and you can imagine how much of a pain this was. Thanks to software like Unbounce and Leadpages, you can simply have a different keyword substituted at certain points in your landing page to make it relevant to what a person clicked on to visit that page.

The interfaces for these software are extremely simple to navigate. As always, if this is your first time doing this, keep it simple and experiment slowly and steadily. Always test multiple versions of your pages and you'll see great results. Let's now take a deeper look at the various elements on the landing page and how you can optimize them.

Landing Page Elements

We don't need to tell you that headlines are important. From the second your visitor lands on your page, you have about two to thirty seconds to make an impression. Granted, this is a pretty wide range but this depends on how much commitment your ad calls for in the first place.

There are many formulas for a great headline, and I'll discuss this in the copywriting section of this chapter. Use one of these proven formulas to hook your reader. Remember to keep it relevant to what they just clicked on. While the subheading or sub headline doesn't get as much attention, it is nonetheless important.

The most important function of the subheading is to convince people to keep reading your copy instead of going back to Google. Furthermore, a good subheading will give people a reason to read your page in detail and explore it instead of skimming through it.

The next thing your reader will notice is the hero shot. It is important to have a good visual hook here. Services-based offers tend to have photos of the person offering the service here or some other image that is connected to the service. Another option is to have a video here. This reduces the visual impact but will increase engagement and keep visitors on your page a bit longer. As always a/b test your options.

Testimonials can be a bit of a problem if you're just starting out. These provide social proof and appeals to the inherent herd mentality in all of us. So how do you generate social proof when you're just starting out? Well, to put it simply, you don't. Simply skip this part.

The more long-winded answer is that while social proof is extremely important for sales, low social proof is actually a detriment to your bottom line (Patel, 2017). If your social proof metrics don't stack up properly and communicate trustworthiness, you'll project an image of yourself being not good enough to back up your claims. Social proof is extremely powerful when used right. If you can't use it right, though, don't use it at all.

The benefits section should be completely customer focused. Too many marketers start talking about themselves and fail to focus on what the client needs. Focus on them entirely and talk about how you'll be solving their problems. If you manage to convince them well enough, their next step will be to click your CTA button.

On the surface of it, this is pretty straightforward. After all, there's only so many things you can have as part of the CTA. However, you really should consider the color of the text of your button. Orange is a great color that has been shown to stand out the most and generally appeals to women (Patel, 2017). Blue is a color that is often used to convey trust and goes well with a lot of backgrounds. Green is often used on cheap and tacky landing pages so stay away from that unless it works for your brand.

There are a lot of moving parts to your landing page, so you will need to test multiple portions of it. Above all else, keep the design simple and don't use more text than you have to. The idea is to keep it simple but not oversimplify things.

How to Write Great Copy

Truth be told, copywriting deserves its own book and is far too complex to be addressed in a single section. However, there have already been multiple books written on the subject, so our task isn't as difficult as it seems on paper. If you're new to copywriting and wondering what the difference is between this and normal writing, well copy simply refers to the stuff you write that sells your product.

There are many professional copywriters who will create a great page for you in no time. If your product has high margins and is a big ticket product, I highly encourage you to invest in a great copywriter. If you don't have the budget, there's no need to worry. Simply follow some proven copywriting formulas and add your words where appropriate.

All great copy ultimately engages the reader emotionally and tells a story well. With this in mind, here are the simplest and most effective copywriting templates you can apply.

Before, After, Bridge

This is a simple formula that works for extremely short form copy, such as a tweet or a Facebook post. The formula is quite simple: Here's the before picture, here's the after picture and here's how to get there, which is what the bridge is. An example of this would be "losing fat is hard. How would you like to lose 15lbs in 2 weeks? #copywritinggenius" (fine, I may be adding some fluff in there).

This formula doesn't translate well on to modern day landing pages or website copy, since it is light on details. To fill this gap, we have the PAS formula.

Problem, Agitate, Solve

PAS works great for medium-length copy such as an email newsletter or a short landing page where you're trying to get people to commit to a small action. The problem portion in this formula is the same as the "before" section in the previous formula. You simply describe the problem that exists.

However, instead of describing the "after," you describe what your reader's life would be like if the problem continued to exist. This is the agitate portion of the formula. Solve refers to the portion where you plug your product and outline the benefits.

PAS is a great framework since it is extremely flexible. You can shorten this to a tweet as well. For example "Stuck eating your shitty food again? Eat another horrible meal OR learn how to cook delicious meals now! Click <<url>> #stillacopywritinggenius."

In its longer form you will need to extoll the benefits of your product a lot more via bullet points or video and so on.

AIDA

AIDA stands for Attention, Interest, Desire, and Action. This is an extremely popular format in the online world since it works so well. Attention is grabbed via your ad and is kept by your compelling headline. Interest is piqued by describing the problems they will face and the solutions that you can give them. Further interest can be generated by providing social proof.

Desire is created by you describing in detail the various benefits of choosing your product or service and action refers to your CTA. All in all, this is a very simple formula to follow and has been used for a long time because it works.

Pick a template from the above options and practice writing copy using them. You'll find that you'll be able to structure professional looking landing pages in no time and that great copywriting is really about marginal improvements.

Chapter 5: Page Analytics

So you've created great copy and your landing page is up. Now all you need to do is wait for clicks and sales ought to roll in! Well, in a perfect world, this is what would happen. In the real world, though, you will find that you'll focus on the bounce rate and constantly wonder why people are leaving your site. Too much of this and Google will penalize you for providing a poor user experience by downgrading your Q score.

The key to figuring out what's going on is to install on page analytics on your website. Google Analytics does a good job of this, but you need something much more powerful than this, and in this chapter you'll see why.

Uploading and Tracking

Before getting into the nitty gritty of analytics, you need to design your page. Remember how I mentioned in the previous chapter that there are tools to help you do this? So why do you need them? Well, Google will constantly monitor your pages' relevance to the terms you are bidding on.

This means that for every term you use, your page has to be relevant for that. You can't bid on strawberries and provide apples, Google will penalize you pretty quickly for that. This is where the landing page creation software comes in to play. Instead of creating hundreds of pages for all of your keywords, simply group them together and create a single page for each group.

The most popular software to do this is Leadpages but my personal favorite is Unbounce, which gives you greater customization. In both cases, the templates are gorgeous and easy to customize. All you do is paste your copy into them and press publish. Now, you sit back and wait for clicks to arrive.

On Site Behavior

As much preparation as you've carried out up to this point, there's no guarantee that people will buy your product. A huge stumbling block is not being able to see what users think of your website or landing page. A good idea before going live is to submit your website to be tested by services such as usertesting.com or userlytics.com, where you can have your landing pages tested by people.

Incorporate this feedback and go live with it. Once live, sign up for a software called Crazy Egg, which is an onsite tracking software. Crazy Egg allows you to see a heat map of your website and page that indicates the places your users clicked or navigated to the most. What's more, you can even choose to record certain sessions of behavior and fine tune your page based on feedback.

Following this initial feedback, you will have to change a few things on your website. This is a pretty straightforward task since all it takes is a few clicks and maybe a little rewording of your copy. The great thing about this sort of tracking is that you can even analyze visits from multiple sources such as Facebook versus Google Ads. This makes optimization a lot easier.

Google Analytics should be your default tracking software to use to track incoming traffic sources and their behavior. Once the clicks start coming in, all you need to do is track conversions and that's it!

Traffic but Zero Conversions?

Welcome to the troubleshooting section. If you never have to read this, I'll be the happiest person in the world. However, the odds are that you will eventually wander over here wondering what on earth is going wrong with your campaigns. Well, the best strategy to deal with problems is to plan ahead and assume they'll occur. The more scenarios you can prepare for, the easier you'll find handling them is.

A common problem is receiving loads of traffic but not seeing any conversions. I wish there was an easy answer for this, but there really isn't. It could depend on a number of things such as but not limited to:

- Bad design
- Bad headlines
- Bad sales copy
- Bad CTAs
- Too many distractions and no clarity (Bad UX)

Before getting into all of these bads, you might be wondering what a good conversion rate is? After all, without a benchmark to hit it's a bit pointless trying to figure out what's good or bad.

According to research performed by Crazy Egg a good landing page converts at an oddly specific 27.4% (Patel, 2017).

These are at the high end, though. On average, landing pages convert somewhere between two to six percent, which sounds abysmal but once you factor in the traffic volumes, these numbers don't look so bad. All in all, you should be aiming for something close to ten percent.

There is another factor in all of this. While your conversion rate forms a good starting point, you should aim to increase it beyond this level. Aiming for an increase of at least one percent per month is a good goal throughout the product life cycle. Now that you know what a good benchmark is, let's get into analyzing your problems.

The first step to being your diagnosis with is the quality of your traffic.

Traffic Quality

Not all traffic is equal, especially the stuff that comes from Google. When you first set up your ad campaigns, your goal will be to generate as much traffic as possible and this is a normal thing to do. As you progress, though, you should pay much more attention to the quality of your traffic.

What do I mean by quality? Well, it begins with your advertising goals. Is your traffic consistent with what you want to achieve? Or are you looking for high quality spenders but attracting bums instead? It comes down to how well you've differentiated your keywords and categorized them in your sales funnel.

A common mistake is to confuse the goals of SEO with ads because the keyword research process is exactly the same. The difference is that SEO focuses on all layers of the funnel while paid ads only focus on the last stages where people are much more likely to buy your product.

Even with this focus, it can be easy to misclassify keywords and get things wrong. So always analyze your individual keywords and check which ones are converting the best and take a look at the poorly performing ones. If you spot obvious differences in performance, then it becomes easy to focus on what is working and put the rest on pause.

Often, all keywords will perform equally poorly and in such cases, you need to dig deeper.

Headlines

Your headline and your USP are the first and obvious places to begin. Is your headline catchy enough or is it disconnected from the rest of your copy? Often, a lot of effort is put into creating a high quality headlines and it sometimes results in a headline that is totally different from the rest of the copy.

A headline that screams with excitement cannot be backed up by copy that is sedate. Check the congruency. Using heat maps, you can see how far down people scroll and where they spend most of their time on your page. Use this to inform your modifications. If you do need to change your headlines, here are some tips:

- Keep it simple and state the proposition up front
- Use questions

- Use tabloid/National Enquirer style headlines

- Use keywords like "FREE," "secret," and so on

- Create a listicle headline or a "how to" headline

Add Social Proof

When starting off, a big reason you'll find no takers for your product due to the fact that your social proof is miscalibrated. As mentioned previously, it is better to have no social proof rather than poor social proof. That being said, it is better to have good social proof compared to none. As much as you are in love with your product, remember you're not the one buying it.

If you have no social proof, your product needs to be truly great. If your product isn't great enough to overcome that barrier, you'll suffer from the lack of people vouching for you. So seek to get as many testimonials as you can. When you do receive testimonials, make sure they describe the service you offered to them clearly and that they describe things in detail.

A lot of products have one word testimonials such as "great!" or "awesome" and so on left by the Brian W's and Tracy H's of this world. This is an example of poor social proof. Stuff like this will hurt your sales and increase your ad costs. So the question remains, how do you generate credible social proof when starting out?

One easy way of doing this is to earn some certifications that are valid in your niche. Given the number of online academies these days, earning a certification is not an expensive proposition. For example, in the world of content marketing, Hubspot offers a number of free certification courses. Other professionals in your field might know it's free, but a large number of your customers won't and adding a badge to your landing page will boost your credibility.

Another great way to increase your profile is to partner with a larger agency of some kind. Again, using Hubspot as an example, you can choose to become one of their sales or marketing agency partner. This will lead to them driving traffic to you as a preferred merchant. This doesn't apply equally to all niches, but it is worth looking into.

Lastly, consider adding credibility to your blog. If you're starting out there as well, instead of pumping out articles for SEO purposes constantly, focus on building backlinks from credible sources. A great way to do this is to interview and shout out influencers in your niche or to highlight them in some way. Once you do this they will likely link back to you and along with traffic, might even be willing to try out your product and leave a testimonial.

After all of this, there are black hat tactics. Now, I'm not saying these are bad because they're not as long as you're genuinely selling a good product. However do not make the mistake of relying on them for too long since over the long term, it's just not worth it. A common way of spoofing social proof is to hire someone from Fiverr to leave you reviews that you wrote yourself.

Just be aware that knowledge of this practice is widespread, and the last thing you want happening is you being called out for using actors to leave reviews.

Redesign Your Lead Form

Often simple and small visual tweaks to your lead capture form will result in huge conversion spikes. There is no set way to go about this, you will simply need to tweak things and see how it works. Either way, the lead gen form is a hotspot on your page and if you notice that you're not receiving too much attention in that area, something is wrong with the design.

An easy fix is to make them small and simple. Don't ask for reams of information, just have your visitors fill out a few boxes at most and get them to click or subscribe. Obviously, this won't work for the buy CTA, but at that point you'll be capturing their emails anyway during the checkout process.

Go Minimalist to the Max

Some landing pages are extremely focused and bare bones. They simply need you to do one particular task, and that's it. Such hyper specific landing pages work great for those instances when you need someone to give you their email or when you need them to sign up to your newsletter in exchange for a lead magnet.

Affiliate marketers can use this one to great effect. Once the user clicks your ad, they will be redirected to your landing page where you can give away your lead magnet in return for their email. Once this is done, simply redirect them to the affiliate product page, which has already been designed to optimize for sales conversions.

This bare bones approach keeps the customer completely focused on what they need to do next and simply follow a few steps. Even if you aren't an affiliate marketer, consider using an intermediary landing page before redirecting people to your website. What's more, a well-designed landing page will minimize your bounce rate.

What I mean is, if you're selling a product and if people don't like it they'll immediately bounce. Placing a landing page in between lessens the probability of bouncing since you'll have them complete a small task before redirecting them. This decreases the probability of you being penalized for low quality scores.

Test Colors and Shapes

I've already mentioned how colors play a role in buying decisions. Orange is generally the best, but the world's biggest shopping engine, Amazon, uses a rather sickly looking yellow color. For whatever reason, this works for them. The ultimate aim with this is to generate contrast between the button's color and the background of your website.

Use a color wheel to determine opposite colors and design your buttons appropriately. Another area you can test is the shape of your CTA buttons. For some reason, we don't like sharp edged buttons and this is why you'll rarely see perfectly sharp edged CTA buttons (Patel, 2017). Often, they'll be rounded or even circular at one end.

Size matters as well. If your CTA button is too small, your reader will skip right past it. If it's too big, it'll simply wreck the design. So play around with it and see what works best.

CTA Text

Once you've got a handle on the shape and color of your CTA buttons, take a look at the text that's in them. Often a simple CTA works well when it's at the end of long copy. However, the preliminary CTA buttons you display should have some explanatory text in them.

For example, saying "Yes, send me my 30 free tips!" is far better than saying "Yes, sign me up!" During the initial portions of your copy, the reader is doing their best to figure out what's going on and what your offer is all about. So make it easy for them by explicitly mentioning it in the CTA. This gives them a good idea of what the benefits are, and they'll take you up on your offer in higher numbers.

Get the language correct as well. A good tip is to write as if you're speaking to just one person instead of an audience. So use language such as "you," "your," "my," etc. instead of alluding to "we."

Make it Easy to Take Action

Clicking a button is easy but answering your readers' questions in real time is not. Often, companies will list a callback number to their sales team in order to address any issues. This does not work anymore. People are not so keen on picking up the phone and talking to a person when trying to research a problem thanks to the online resources available.

Therefore, to avoid losing a customer thanks to their questions not being answered, install a chatbot on your website. A tool like Olark is a great addition to your website and will help improve functionality. A lot of the stuff can be automated even though, obviously, more complicated questions will take longer to respond to and will need human intervention.

This also works in an interesting way when it comes to building trust. With data privacy issues on the rise, people are far less comfortable giving out personal information to websites that can use that to track them. A chatbot doesn't need such information, and the act of giving something away for free builds trust with your customers. You'll find that a lot of them will come back to you for more.

Add Cues

This particular tip has to be proof that humans are the most hackable things walking around on the planet. It sounds ridiculous, but data repeatedly shows that it works (Patel, 2017). Have you ever noticed how the images of items or people in ads direct your gaze toward a particular spot?

It doesn't even have to be an arrow. Simply having an image within the ad pointing in one direction or having the person in it look in a certain direction has the power to get us to direct our gaze toward that side of the ad. And what will you find there? Yup! The CTA.

I personally have a hard time believing I can be manipulated like this, but who really knows? The fact is that this technique works and if you still have doubts, go take a look at still ads of Geico.

Notice which way the Gecko's eyes are looking? How about his (its?) hands?

Chapter 6: Setting Up Your Campaign

So here we are finally! After all of that preliminary work and knowledge, here is where you will finally learn to set up your campaign in Google Ads and start gathering data. This chapter might be anticlimactic for some because a lot of the interesting stuff has been covered with regard to the options available to you.

However, ensuring you setup your campaign in line with your design is crucial for success. So, let's take a look at how you go about setting things up.

Campaign Setup

You will need to give your campaign a name, and once this is done you will be prompted to select the targeting location. I've already covered what to do here. Simply enter the location where the greatest number of your customers live, which often happens to be the United States unless you're selling a particular niche product.

Make sure that you deselect the display network choice since you want to only target search results. Once initial data is collected, you can choose to advertise on the display network. Enter your keyword. Google will give you a number of suggestions, but ignore these. You will have done your keyword research by now and will have a full list ready to go. Enter your keywords into the box.

Next, you will need to enter a bid for these group of keywords. Remember how you set your maximum budget per day and your max CPC in a previous chapter? Well, this should give you a fair idea of how much to bid. Remember that there are other factors that Google takes into account when it comes to deciding which ad to show. So don't sweat it if your bid is on the lower side.

Now comes the time for you to decide on the structure of your account. Remember we looked at campaigns, ad sets, and individual ads previously and how they relate to one another? Well, hopefully you've decided on the structure by now. If not, here are some additional suggestions for you to try out.

Structure Types

The first structure to setup your campaigns is based on match type. Match type simply refers to the type of keyword matches you're looking for in your campaigns. So you'll set one up for broad matches, another for phrase matches, and a third for exact matches. You can repeat keywords within these campaigns if you wish and whether you should do that or not really comes down to what niche you're in. As always, test to see what works and then move forward with the things that give the best results.

This method of structuring your campaigns helps if you have a small number of keywords, but if you have a large brand and are looking to invest a significant amount on Google Ads then this sort of a structure won't fit you. Instead, you should separate your campaigns on the basis of brand names or demographics.

However, the large majority of advertisers fall in the middle somewhere, and for such people the best option is to use what are called Single Keyword Ad Groups or SKAGs. This is where you will create separate ad groups for every single keyword in your campaign. In other words, you'll have a separate ad for each keyword.

The SKAG approach requires work since you'll have to maintain each keyword individually but with some careful choices of keywords and the correct match types, you'll be able to laser focus your ads and manage to get clicks for the related search words to it. However, there are huge benefits to this approach that are undeniable.

The first is that your ads will automatically be relevant to the keyword. A common problem that occurs with traditional setup of campaigns is that a single ad has to cover and be relevant for a bunch of keywords. This can be tough to do and achieving relevance across all keywords is not guaranteed. The SKAG eliminates this problem since you have one keyword per ad, and therefore relevance and quality scores should not be a problem.

One implication of higher quality scores is improved CTRs since you're not laser focused on what the customer is searching for. Once your CTRs start increasing, everything else improves including your impressions, your CPC's, your average positions and so on. In other words, your campaigns becomes far more efficient.

Also, further down the line, they'll help improve the efficiency of your retargeting campaigns. All in all, SKAGs are a great way to organize your campaigns but the question is should you do it? Is the tradeoff between increased work and potentially greater conversions worth it? Well, this depends on how much you're willing to put into your campaigns. At some point you will experience diminishing returns since the keyword list will simply become too big.

Therefore, it helps to really understand what your customer's intent is and to segment your ad sets on that basis. This is not an easy thing to do and you will make mistakes at first, but this is fine. Choose as many broad match keywords at first to take care of variations and then look at the search term report to see what works and what doesn't. This process has been covered previously.

Whichever structure you use make sure you balance the demands on your time and the return on your investment well. You don't want to be the person sitting in front of their screen all day tweaking their campaigns looking to squeeze a few more dollars out of them. Designing your ad sets optimally is a key piece to this puzzle.

Writing The Ad

Writing your ad is as straightforward as putting your USP in a single sentence to your customer. In other words, not straightforward at all. There are many elements that go into a great one-line pitch and if you try to hit each and every single one of them, you're likely to overcomplicate things.

Instead, simply follow the eight tips in the sections below and you'll ensure your ad copy converts well and will always be relevant to your customer.

Keywords, Keywords

Imagine you order a sub at a sandwich shop, and it's one of those places where your order gets called out. If the person behind the counter simply yells "Six-inch sub" when your order is ready, you wouldn't know what they're talking about, would you? This is the same thing as using keywords in ads that are different from what the user searched for.

The SKAG structure eliminates this but if you're not using this, try to keep your ad copy as close to the keyword as possible. Use it exactly as someone would search for it, and you'll get better responses. Don't stuff your keywords into the copy since this will result in a penalty in the form of a lower Q score. Write it as naturally as you can, and the rest will follow.

Also, make sure your keyword is prominently present in your landing page. This means your headline, at the very least, should have the keyword. In addition to this, incorporate it into your subheading as well as preliminary copy. Don't stuff keywords beyond this since it might not come across as natural sounding. Even if you can't naturally incorporate your keyword into the sub header, don't worry. As long as your headline has the keyword, you'll be fine.

Check for Specificity

The ad copy for your keywords that are broad in nature, like "cocktail dresses," can be less specific in nature since this is what the user is searching for. However, the more specific their search query is, the more you want to reflect that throughout your ad.

The most obvious place to do this is to modify your headline to include the exact keyword.

So if someone searched for "women's red cocktail dress" have this exact phrase show up in the headline. Next, repeat the phrase in the ad copy somewhere. Also, don't forget to modify the little green link that shows up beneath the headline in your ad. This needs to be the same URL as your landing page and can therefore be fully customized.

Reflecting the level of specificity back to your user is a great way to get them to click on your ad since it gives the impression that you know exactly what they're looking for, and you have exactly what they want.

Check Your CTAs

People often assume that just because a user sees an ad, they'll automatically click on it. Well, this might be the case with you personally but generally speaking, people will never take action unless they're prompted to do so. Also, your CTA in the ad should reflect what is on the landing page.

For example, if your ad CTA said "learn more" but your landing page is a short page that is pushing them to buy your product, you won't get too many conversions since the intent is all off. The ad copy CTA is also a great way to get your user to prequalify themselves.

Prequalifying refers to filtering out those users who are unlikely to buy your product but will click on your ad anyway, costing you money. By setting up a hurdle of some kind, you get those unwilling to put the effort to filter themselves out. A CTA such as

"Book Luxury Tours" will weed out those people who are not interested in this option.

Play With Psychology

This is the toughest part to get right since it can be difficult to separate your own thought processes from that of your ideal customer. You'll figure it out through trial and error. Prequalifying is an example of using psychology to filter out desirable customers from the crowd.

Another tactic is to highlight the benefits of the product. Using an extension to highlight social proof, via reviews, is another tactic. Sometimes, you can try to use negative headlines. These require more experience to pull off since it can be tough to get the tone right. If you get it wrong, you'll likely turn people off.

The easiest method is to simply highlight the solution and benefit the user will receive by clicking your ad. You should know what problem you're addressing so just highlight this and add social proof and let your landing page do the rest.

Follow Through

This one should go without saying but always under-promise and over-deliver. Do not make claims you can't back up or you will be skewered down the line. Remember that social proof is the most powerful way of selling stuff online since people cannot interact face to face with you. Therefore, what others say about you is the primary method of evaluation your buyer will use.

Always back your claims and follow through on any service you offer. Do not risk losing your reputation by making tall claims, no matter the short term marketing benefit that will provide you with.

Use Extensions

Google gives you a ton of extensions to use, and these are extremely powerful especially if you're a small or local business. Here's the full list of extensions you can choose from:

1. Sitelink

2. Callout

3. Structured Snippet

4. Call

5. Message

6. Location

7. Affiliate Location

8. Price

9. App

10. Promotion

If you're a local business, which ones do you think you should use? Well, it's simple, isn't it? Call, message, location, and price are the most powerful ones for small businesses. This is what will help you stand out from the big boys. The first three are applicable to all types of businesses, and you should use them as default.

There is a danger of overloading your ad with extensions, so how do you determine what is the right amount? Well, use your competitors as a starting point. See what extensions they have and increase your extensions by a little so that it stands out. Above all else, make sure you're not sacrificing readability for your user.

Dynamic Ad Features

These are a neat basket of features that Google gives you when you create your ad. The first dynamic feature you're presented with is keyword insertion feature. The choices are not explicit so you need to type "{" into the keyword title box to trigger the dropdown that gives you the choices.

Keyword insertion allows you to replace portions of your title with alternative keywords. In other words, you can use the same ad copy for two keywords and Google will substitute the second keyword in place of the first in the second copy.

The second dynamic feature is even more powerful in that you can create if/then loops within your ads to decide whether they ought to display or not. If your user is on a mobile device, you can change your CTA to read "call us" instead of having them fill out a form. You can even create offers for specific users. For example, mobile users get a special code they can use on checkout and so on.

Lastly, speaking of special offers, you can create countdowns for when your offer will expire and Google will keep updating your ad copy to reflect the urgency.

All of these options are a great way to boost your ad performance. Keep this in mind when writing your ad copy. Remember, it's just a few lines so don't overthink it. Simply state the benefit and let Google do the rest for you. Always keep your landing page copy consistent with everything you've promised.

A common pitfall is to customize offers for a particular user group but not have the landing page reflect that. This will hit your Q score massively, so don't attempt to get fancy right off the bat. Take it easy with slow steps, and you'll slowly build your expertise at this.

Once your ad copy is done, it is time to take a look at the things that come next. First, you'll need to carry out some basic house cleaning and maintenance to ensure everything is setup correctly and you haven't made some mistakes during the setup process. Let's take a look at all of this stuff in the next section.

Post Ad Maintenance

The first thing you need to do is setup conversion tracking within Google. This is a pretty simple thing to do. All you do is head over to the tools menu on top and click on "conversions." Once you're there, you need to select the "website" option and enter all the details, like the URL etc. Remember to add the URL of the page, which your customer will see upon checkout or after taking the action you want.

Google will give you a snippet of code and you add this to your page's backend and you'll be able to track conversions right from your ads dashboard. Speaking of the dashboard, it's a good idea to pause your ad for a while and take a look at the way things are set up. Check things such as the keyword match type and the budget and so on.

After this you need to maintain the ad as discussed previously. Google will review your ad, and you'll see its status being updated after an hour or so. If this is your first ad, it might take a little longer. How often should you be checking in? Well, there's no template for this.

My advice is to check in every day to see how things are going at first. Once you get a feel for the number of clicks you're getting per ad or ad set, you'll figure out how often things need to be changed. Remember, the first portion of your ad campaign strategy is to merely test what works. So remember to a/b test your ad copy, and you can also run multiple keyword sets in different ads. Keep your budget as low as possible before expanding it with whatever works best.

Here's a tip: as your campaigns mature you'll see in phrases and keywords in the search term report that sound like robot searches. These will usually look like "cocktail dress women red women green women blue" and so on. No human will ever type or even ask Google this sort of a thing via voice search. As these terms keep cropping up, paste them into your negative keywords list since robot searches are not looking to buy anything from you and are wasted clicks.

A good CTR to aim for is around eight percent. Remember your CTR is different from your conversion rate, and, ultimately, it is your conversion rates that matter. Here are some simple things to look at when it comes to boosting your CTR.

Time of Day

This is usually a big factor in CTR rates. You might have some preconceived notions about when your users search for you, but the reality might be different. So review when you're receiving the most clicks and allocate more budget to it by using the time of day modifier. Simply stop displaying your ad during those times when your CTR is low.

Location

Locations are a good thing to a/b test, and I'll talk all about this in the next chapter. In terms of improving your CTR, check to see which areas are giving you the best performance. Can you reduce the area size? For example, if you chose United States at first but are seeing that Floridians and New Yorkers are your best customers, run ads only in those regions and boost your returns.

All in all, monitor these key metrics during the first month. It'll take this long for you to see results so keep an eye on these things:

- CPC

- Cost per conversion

- Number of conversions

- Number of clicks

- CTR

In addition to this, here are some common things to watch out for and what to do about them:

1. My budget has been hit on the first day–If this happens, you're bidding to high. Lower your bids for the top costing ones or all of them, if costs were distributed.

2. My budget was barely spent on the first day–Increase your bids by 40% at the very least and check back tomorrow for further adjustments. Aim to have around 10% left in the tank at the end of the day at all times in terms of budget.

3. My ads are too low after a week of running them–Increase your bids by 25% if your budget allows it. If not, cancel the ad and start over.

4. I'm not getting enough clicks–First reduce the CPC bids for the high-costing ones. Next, research new keywords from the search term report. Lastly, pause your high CPC keywords. You should do this only at the weekly mark and not before that.

5. Some of my ads suck, I don't know what I was thinking–This happens more than you might imagine. Don't delete ads during the first month as much as possible. However, delete the obviously bad ones with extremely low CTRs like 1% or less. Sometimes a few bad keywords bring down the entire campaign. Pause these low CTR ones and see if it makes a difference.

You will run into these problems repeatedly during the first month so play around with the steps recommended above to see if they make a difference. Don't be in a hurry to optimize. Usually, it takes a week to have some level of decent data, so wait for at least that long to see how things go.

A handy template for review is to check in at the twenty-four hour mark, weekly, fourteen days, twenty-one days, and monthly. Hence, after the first day of going live, check in roughly every week to make modifications and to check how things are going.

Chapter 7: A/B Testing

What if you could run experiments on your ads to see which one works best and then choose the one that delivers the best performance? This is exactly what a/b experimentation allows you to do, and Google Ads gives you the ability to do this easily.

If you've ever dabbled in online advertising before this, you know the importance of a/b testing. The fact is that there are so many variables involved that setting up your ad can be a daunting process. Within Google ads itself there are so many options when it comes to testing your ads.

There's the headline, the URL, the text, the extension, the modifier and so on. Which ones really matter and what is the thing that is really driving sales. In response to all these pleas, Google finally delivered a solution within AdWords that helps you experiment to your heart's content and deploy your money effectively.

Variations

After debuting in 2017, Google Ads Variations have become extremely popular and an easy way to a/b test your ads for maximum effectiveness. The fact is that split testing your ads is something that you should do, but you will not beyond a few basic actions. You might setup an alternative ad and once you have a decent response from one of them, you might move ahead with one and disable the other.

I you're starting out, you'll likely have both ads perform badly and need to start over. Whatever your situation, the fact is that constant testing is what makes ad campaigns successful. Without this, you're moving from firing into the dark to firing into semi darkness.

Setting up Experiments

To set up variations you first need to have adopted the new UI that was rolled out by Google. If you are still sticking to the old UI because you love how clunky it is, chances are you're missing out on a lot of new features (Finn, 2018). Anyway, head over to your main menu on the left and scroll all the way down to the "drafts and experiments" option.

Once you click on this, you'll open a new page that will have three options presented. Click the "ad variations" option and create a new variation. When starting out with this, I recommend creating a single variation for a single campaign. Like the rest of Google ads, there's a danger of running away with yourself and getting lost in the complexity of things. So keep it simple.

One thing to note is that Google will not let you create multiple variations of a single campaign. So you're limited to just one per campaign. Once you're presented with creating a new variation, you'll be presented with a bunch of filters that allow you to play around with all kinds of things.

Despite the large number of filters, there are three types of methods Google allows you to use to create a variation within your ads. These are find and replace, update text, and swap headlines. The method by which each of these work is not terribly complicated. Find and replace simply refers to finding and replacing a particular portion of your ad copy with a variation.

Update text allows for more wholesale changes to your copy while swap headlines allows you to replace one headline with another. Once you've finalized this option, it's time to start running your variations to see how they work. These variations allow you to play around with tiny details in your ads that have a huge impact.

A good place to use them is within your CTA. Play around with the text in there. Perhaps "buy now" can be better replaced with "grab your copy," and so on. This is why variations are so powerful. As you might have noticed thus far, variations don't lend themselves well to split testing early in your campaign. This is a technique you want to use once your campaigns have grown mature and you wish to enhance their optimization.

In case you wish to learn about split testing in the beginning, well, the good news is that the metric I'll be talking about in the following sections are the same ones that you need to track in the early split tests. The only difference is in terms of setup. For mature campaigns, you'll be using the variations option but or young campaigns you'll simply create different ads within ad sets and monitor them separately.

Having got that out of the way, let's move on.

Tracking and Confirming

Once you've done the initial setup it's time to name the variation and specify the proportion of your budget you wish to allocate to this variation. A good proportion is 50/50. As for naming, just use your common sense and name it something that you can spot easily. Often people give these variations obscure names, and this only complicates things when you want to optimize them.

Once the data starts rolling in, it's simply a matter of looking at which one is performing better and going with the more efficient one. A word of caution here. Google presents you with three options on screen when the time comes to adopt a variation in favor of an original ad.

The second option, which is titled "remove original ads and create new ads with this variation" should be avoided at all costs! Do not click on this. The reason is that once you do this, Google deletes the data you've received from these old ads and replaces it with the new ones. This data is valuable, so don't outright delete it.

Instead, pause your old ads or keep running them side by side the new ones as a continued split test. The same advice applies to split tests conducted at early stages. The data within them is valuable, so do not delete the ones that performed poorly. Simply deactivate them. This way you can come back to them at a later point to see if you can change something to optimize them in some manner.

Now that the technical stuff is out of the way, let's look at what things you ought to be split testing in your ads.

What to Split Test

Split testing is a venue where most people become aware of the awesome power in their hands. You have the ability to test everything everywhere at every single point in time. So how do you stop yourself from getting buried under mountains of data points? First off, understand that as you get better at this, you'll automatically know what to do and which parts to split test.

For now, though, as a beginner, simply focus on testing a few key areas. Luckily, there are some effective templates for you to follow. So let's look at them one by one.

CTA

This is an obvious thing to split test. Playing around with the words in your CTA has massive implications for your conversions and your CTRs. Set up experiments to see which action verb works better. Research suggests that "get" works the best (Dane, 2019) while "click" works the worst.

Play around with the placement of your CTA too. Instead of placing it right at the end of your ad copy, try placing it right in front and then continuing with the rest of your copy. The more you play around with this, the greater your chances are of optimizing your CTRs.

Play The Emotional Game

Should you go positive or negative? Is it better to highlight how amazing your product is or to ask your customer how bad things are right now and present your product as a solution. There's no easy answer to this, and the only way to find out is to experiment.

Generally speaking, positive sentiment works best but it's not as if it's a runaway winner.

Sometimes negative sentiment works wonders as well. The point is that the worst thing that can happen with your ad is that people remain indifferent. Indifference is the same as irrelevant as far as you're concerned.

Change the Philosophy

Generally, all ad copy falls into one of two categories: features or benefits. Some copywriters swear by listing the features, especially for tech savvy audiences while others lay down their lives upon the altar of benefits. Both of them are effective and again, playing around with either option helps determine what your audience likes.

Each audience behaves differently, so don't assume one philosophy that has worked in one niche to automatically work in another. Always experiment and keep testing constantly to get the best results.

Guidelines

Despite repeated warnings, it is easy for you to get lost in the world of split testing. With this in mind, I've written this section to serve as a framework of best practices for you to follow. You don't need to do everything on here, but doing the majority of them should give you good results. More importantly, your results will be relevant.

#1-Test One Thing

Your split test should aim to test just one variable against another. Do not ever combine multiple variables into a single test. If you do this, you won't know which one is working and which one is having the greater effect or why. Simple and obvious really, but you'd be surprised at how easy it is to fall foul of this.

#2- Test the Most Important Stuff

There are a lot of things for you to potentially test. If you were to drill down and test each and every single one of them, it's going to take you forever to come up with results and you'll be split testing for the rest of your life. Hence, focus on the things that have the biggest impact on your bottom line. The CTA is a good example of this.

Other things that fall into this category are your headlines, your price, USP, landing pages and images. Another important thing to split test is your choice of bidding strategy. Keep it simple here and test manual versus automatic, instead of splitting automatic strategies. Whichever gives you the best result, go with that.

#3- Test the Stuff You Want to Improve

What are the areas of your campaign that are lagging? You might be receiving great conversions but you'd like to go for more, so what is it that is holding you back? Determining which area to improve can be a slippery slope since it can be difficult to isolate what is really causing your results.

This is even more so the case when things are going well. In such instances, the last thing you want to do is to unwittingly undo things that do work. I mean, if everything is rubbish, it's easy to decide what to change, isn't it? Take the time to try to isolate what seems to be holding your results back and then run experiments on it.

This will take some time to do, so you need to drill down deeply into your data and check the patterns. There's no template for this kind of stuff, and you'll learn mostly through experience.

#4- Aim for Statistical Significance

Statistical significance is such an important part of split testing, I cannot overemphasize it. Think of it as the lifeblood of your split tests. Your variation might have received greater clicks than your original ad, but how long has it been running? What level of clicks are statistically significant?

There are a lot of variables that go into this decision, so you need to examine as many as possible. One common variable is seasonality. If you unwittingly run a variation in August when everyone is outside enjoying the last few minutes of sunshine, the clicks you receive are not going to be great. So despite the number of clicks you get, you might want to run it a little longer.

Another common variable is a special event of an offer in a complementary product that is driving clicks to your ad. The best way to determine a statistically significant level is to map out all the variables in advance as best as possible. Generally, two weeks to a month is a good enough time to collect enough data.

I'd be hesitant to place a number of clicks to use for this metric since your aim is to maximize them.

#5- Get Granular

This one goes back to organizing the structure of your campaigns but conduct your split tests at the lowest level possible. If you start creating new campaigns every single time you want to split test something, you're going to create a bunch of one ad headaches for yourself.

Instead isolate and test repeatedly and keep them as low as possible in terms of account structure.

#6- Rinse and Repeat

So you've found the best possible combinations and variations and are at the top of your niche. Congratulations! Enjoy all five minutes of your time at the top. The thing is that your competitors are not going to sit back and simply let you stay on top. The only way to remain there is to keep testing and keep modifying.

This is where old fashioned elbow grease beats out fancy tech. Your competitor might have more money and more know-how, but with hard work and consistent testing, you'll be able to compete with them on level terms. This applies especially to small, local businesses.

While Google prefers larger organizations when it comes to organic search results, the fact is that within paid ads, it actually prefers smaller businesses since these tend to be more relevant to the customer. So don't slack on your efforts.

Keep repeating your testing over and over!

Chapter 8: Remarketing

Let's say someone clicks on your ad and visits your website. They like your product but just happen to be in the wrong stage of your funnel to actually make a purchase right now. Or let's say that your product is an impulse purchase but for whatever reason, right before checking out, they had to leave to do something else and forgot about it.

Should you tamely let such people go away? Of course not! Targeting these people is what remarketing is all about, and Google enables you to do this throughout their network of websites.

In this chapter, we'll look at remarketing strategies and how you can use them to boost your conversions.

Remarketing Strategies

First let's look at the different types of remarketing strategies that exist. These can be listed as:

1. Standard remarketing

2. Dynamic remarketing

3. Mobile app remarketing

4. Search ad lists remarketing

5. Video remarketing

6. Email list remarketing

Remarketing, as you can see, allows you to follow your customer as they travel along the web from one site to another across Google's ad network. This is what makes Google ads so powerful. On other platforms, such as Facebook, once the user leaves, you don't have strong ways of continuing to target them. However, Google gives you unprecedented access to this.

Let's look at these one by one briefly. Standard remarketing allows you to show banner ads on the display network once users leave your site. The way it works is this. Once a visitor arrives at your site, Google places a cookie in their browser, which contains information about the fact that visited your site. Once they bounce from your site to another website on Google's network, they will see banner ads on those external websites advertising your product.

Dynamic remarketing kicks things up a notch. Let's say a visitor to your site made it all the way to the product page and viewed an item. With dynamic remarketing, you can show that item they viewed across all sites on Google's network instead of showing a generic ad as with standard remarketing. Sometimes, this can backfire since people bounced for a reason and will find your constant ads annoying.

However, dynamic ads have a great ROI because people bounce for all kinds of reasons. As you'll see later, you can set time filters on how often you can display such ads to the user. Mobile app remarketing applies if you have an app. In such cases, Google will show an ad for your app on another app the user is on or on other mobile websites they visit. As such, we won't be dealing with this here.

Next up we have search ad lists remarketing or RLSA (remarketing lists for search ads). Whichever naming convention you prefer, this strategy allows you to target customers on the search network by showing them custom ads. Video remarketing is becoming more powerful by the day, and I'll cover this in a separate chapter as part of YouTube marketing.

However, the premise is the same. Someone who interacted with or viewed your YouTube channel can be advertised to across the display and search network. Lastly, we have email list remarketing. If you have a list of emails of your customers, you can target them across the network, serving them ads in Gmail, Google Ads and YouTube along with the display network as well. Now you know why emails are still so valuable!

A Word of Caution

Given the amount of work you need to do to setup your initial campaigns, it can be difficult to sit down and hammer out a remarketing strategy. You still need to pay a lot of attention to this part since this is where you will either gain more loyal customers or lose potentially loyal ones. Just think about what remarketing really is for a second: You're literally stalking them as they move around the web.

If the visitor does not like your product or if you harass them too much, you're liable to convert a borderline customer into someone who actively avoids you. This is why it is very important to keep in mind that your target is to target those people who have shown interest in your product as opposed to targeting everyone who clicked onto your page by mistake.

Remarketing strategies follow the same path as normal campaigns. You need to strategize, set up, monitor, and optimize them. There are a lot of possibilities as you'll see in this chapter but my advice, as always, is to keep things simple and take things one at a time. Master one sort of targeting and then move to the next.

A good place to start is with email retargeting since every website collects emails as part of business. Use this to highlight some exciting new products or services and you'll build your repeat customer base. Over time, you won't even need to advertise to such people since they'll keep coming back. It might sound strange to say this but the ultimate goal of all advertising is to reduce the need to advertise.

Now that the Yoda like portion of this chapter is finished, move on to practical stuff, we shall!

Setting Up Remarketing Campaigns

Your first step is to decide which actions deserve remarketing campaigns. The most obvious one is to target people who reached a particular step in a process but didn't follow through. A good example of this is someone who didn't complete the checkout process. Another strategy is to target people who viewed a portion of your website but didn't view another.

So if you're selling cocktail dresses and shoes, why not retarget the customer who bought just one product but not the other? Once you've decided this, you can then figure out which pages need to have the remarketing tag. The remarketing tag is what allows Google to install a cookie on the device of the person accessing your website.

My advice is to simply install the tag across all pages of your website. This way, you'll be able to take advantage of all types of remarketing campaigns. Here's how you set up your tag.

Initial Setup

There are two ways of generating a remarketing tag. The first is to do it within AdWords itself. In the main menu, you click "shared library" and then select "audiences" in the new menu that pops up. At this point, you'll be notified that Google doesn't detect a tag on your website. Click "tag details" and navigate your way through it. You'll soon see two links, one tag for websites and another for mobile apps.

Install the website tag across all pages. If you're unsure how to do this simply email your dev support team or the support team of your theme if you're on WordPress and have them do it for you.

The second method is to do it from within Google Analytics. Click on the "admin" option on the main menu on the left and then click on "audience definition," which will be available in the second column of the new menu that will be displayed. Once you click this, click on audience → new audience, and here you get to directly create a remarketing list.

The second method is easier since you don't need to update any code on your website to create a list. The only caveat is that you should maintain an active Google Ads account for this to work.

Next Steps

Once your initial code and lists are created, you can go about fleshing out the various options within them. Within Google Ads, you can access the same menu as in Analytics where you can build your audience list. The options are exactly the same in both cases, so let's walk through them.

Once you click on the "shared library" option as previously, you'll see the audience lists section. Click on this and under the remarketing tab, you'll see a "+" sign that allows you to create a new list. You'll have options here to target website visitors, app users, YouTube viewers, or email list subscribers. Let's stick with website users for now.

The menu that comes up allows you to define an audience name and the particular URL they need to navigate to be targeted. An example is a list named "cart abandoned," which refers to people adding things to their cart and not checking out. You can retarget these people by showing them ads reminding them of the products they liked and so on.

You'll be prompted to enter a value for the membership duration. This is simply how long you want the cookie that's installed on their device to be active. The highest value is 540 days. The value that you choose should be in line with your strategy and who you're targeting. For example, if you're trying to target abandoned shopping carts, reminding them beyond a month is pretty pointless.

Next, you can also set the frequency cap, which refers to how many times you want these people to be shown your ad. Again, this needs to be in line with your strategy. You can set limits per day, week, month, etc.

Setting things up is pretty basic when it comes to remarketing. The really good stuff happens when you start creating custom combinations and combining them with membership durations to create a delayed targeting strategy. We'll look at this in the next section.

Optimization

The first optimization strategy you can run is to create a custom audience, which can be a combination of the options within the audience selection menu. This is not the only way to build a custom audience. You can target users who went through a particular workflow as well.

For example, you can target people who hit the checkout button but never reached the order confirmation page. In other words, they got lost somewhere in between. You can also build custom audiences for similar workflows using your YouTube audience or app audience. The possibilities are endless, so you really need to think about what your aim is with you retargeting campaigns.

One great way of leveraging custom audiences is to utilize the membership duration option to target people at different stages of your funnel. Let's say someone was introduced to your brand thirty days ago and someone else was introduced 180 days ago. The messaging you will need to include in your ads will need to differ for both sets of people.

Hence, creating a custom audience based on the membership duration is a great way to segment your audience and target them. You can drill down further into these individual audiences by setting up retargeting options based on their actions on your website.

Retargeting can get complicated real fast so here are some simple ways to enhance the efficiency of your campaigns. These can also serve as retargeting templates.

Advanced Lists

You can leverage the full power of Google analytics with your remarketing campaigns and use this data to segment your audience efficiently. Analytics tracks a number of data points with regard to your visitors and some of these include pages visited, time spent on site, geography, demographics, traffic source and so on.

Setting up specific campaigns to target these people could keep them coming back. It's no secret that people from one source will behave differently from another. With custom audience retargeting there is no cap to how you can slice and dice your audiences and then use that increase your profits.

Another great way to build your lists is to categorize them on the basis of where they are in your funnel. I would say this is imperative for you to do. If your website has a blog, you can segment people who visited your content pages but haven't explored your product pages to nudge them toward a sale.

A second option is to target holiday purchasers or special event purchasers. Set up a retargeting window of a year and serve them ads that remind them that it's time to buy something for that time of the year.

Ad Types

Google offers the option of a number of ad formats such as lightbox ads, video ads, etc. Each type has certain advantages over the other, and you should play around with them to see which one fits you best. Lightbox ads tend to have high engagement because commitment is established before the user clicks the ad.

In case you're not aware how a lightbox ad works, the user hovers over the image and a few seconds later, the lightbox appears with your ad message. The user has already indicated interest in the ad and has therefore spent some time, no matter how little, engaging with the ad. This makes them more likely to click through it.

A powerful option Google gives you is Gmail ads. As the name suggests, these are targeted ads show in people's inboxes. With Gmail being the largest email service provider, and with people having multiple accounts, Gmail ads do pretty well. On the opposite end of the spectrum we have video ads.

These are possibly the most annoying ads in existence and show up on YouTube. Given the slickness of advertising on other platforms, YouTube's integration methods invoke the dark ages are a prime example of how not to engage an audience. I'll discuss all of this in a separate chapter, but I don't recommend running YouTube ads for a variety of reasons.

One of the big reasons for this is that viewer dissatisfaction on YouTube is far higher than with other platforms. From the broken recommended for you section to updates making the interface clunkier, it's safe to say that YouTube survives solely because of Google's heft standing behind it that prevents competitors from taking it out back and putting it out of its misery, as it deserves.

Whatever you think of my rant, the fact is that YouTube exists and you need to use it. However, don't use it in the traditional manner to advertise.

Lastly, we have general purpose ads that allow you to showcase your products. These are extremely effective when targeted well and building a custom audience around this can be very useful.

Smart Dynamic Remarketing

Dynamic remarketing is one of the most powerful advertising options Google gives you, and you should seek to leverage this as much as possible. Within the dynamic remarketing umbrella, there are three strategies you can employ which are extremely effective.

The first of these is managed placement on the display network. Let's say you're selling flowers and want to target people who have bounced from your site. Let's imagine that one of these people is a man who wishes to buy flowers for his significant other but decides to put it off for some reason. After bouncing, he decides to visit a digital marketing website or blog.

Would it make sense for your flower shop ads to show up on such a website? While it might garner a laugh from this man when he sees your ad, overall it looks a bit incompetent. This is why remarketing is a double-edged sword. You should do it only if you can do it efficiently, which is why strategizing in advance is so important.

The smart way to target this person would be to advertise when he visits sites where an ad for a flowers seems more congruent. An e-Commerce site or a blog that lists gift recommendations for occasions or anything else you can think of. Exclude the ones that don't make sense and bid only on the ones that do.

The next strategy is called threshold remarketing and this involves segmenting your visitors on the basis of the price of the item they viewed. If you're selling stuff all the way from $5 to $1000, the person who is looking to buy the $1000 item is going to behave and react differently from the one shopping for the $5 item. What's more, the same person will behave differently depending on what they're shopping for.

You can choose to serve different ads to people on the basis of what they've looked at by using the "ecomm_totalvalue" variable within your lists setup page (Dane, 2019). This way you make your ads more targeted and efficient. The last strategy is to utilize time as described previously.

People who have abandoned carts or haven't checked out and so on can be reminded of their products via targeted ads. Using dynamic remarketing you can showcase those products to them, and this will serve as a handy reminder to such people.

Smart Usage of RLSAs

The RLSA is a very powerful method of remarketing because of the ability to layer it within your existing campaigns. This way, you can whittle down audiences for certain ads that have converted well for you and you can increase their conversion rates by targeting those you know have already taken action in the past.

The danger with RLSA campaigns is that it is easy to exclude potential buyers by applying too extreme a filter to your audiences. As always your strategizing sessions should inform whether you need to branch your RLSE out into a separate campaign or layer it into an existing one.

Chapter 9: YouTube Marketing

I've been giving YouTube the short shrift thus far in this book because, quite frankly, ads are not integrated well into the platform at all. This doesn't mean YouTube ads are completely useless. For certain niches it can work very well. Traditional retail is a good example of this.

The problem with YouTube, as I've mentioned earlier, is that it has the most dissatisfied audience on the web. Most of the time discussions around YouTube involve the bizarre recommendations it throws up and the non-ergonomic updates it releases. With every update, YouTube makes its interface more complex while Google goes the other way and streamlines things.

Does this mean marketing on YouTube is a waste of time? Hardly. You must understand that paid ads are a small portion of the marketing game when it comes to YouTube. In fact, a lot of what I'll show you in this chapter will only go to serve your YouTube inbound content strategy.

So before we begin, it is crucial that you already have a YouTube channel with content on it. If you're starting out, then you'll see no ROI on YouTube ads. It's better to focus on paid Google search and pumping out regular content on YouTube. So with that cleared up, let's get into it.

Ad Basics

YouTube is the second largest search engine in the world behind its big brother Google. It is also the reason why software like AdBlock exists (Cassidy, 2018). Given the video format of the platform, it can be extremely annoying to have some random person's ad popup before your selected video plays. Even worse are the midstream ads that play. All of this pales in comparison to the special hell that is a non-skippable ad playing midstream.

A lot of content creators simply turn off monetization even when they're eligible since playing ads actively hurts their engagement. Besides, the true method of monetizing YouTube is to take that traffic onto your website and redirect it to your product. Organic marketing on YouTube is far better than paid ads. However, you should run a few paid ads once your channel has enough content on it since this can help you grow your subscriber base. Just don't run any ads on your channel since given YouTube's propensity to screw things up they might end up playing your competitor's ads on your channel!

Let's now take a look at your ad format options.

TrueView Ads

Despite the cutesy name, I'm going to refer to these as the skippable ads. These are the least annoying ones and actually have the highest engagement rates of all formats on YouTube. Why is this? Well, a cleverly designed skippable ad can capture attention and once the main video is done playing, users often go back and check out the brand in the ad they skipped.

This sort of ad also gets to the point quickly with the CTA being frontloaded. In other words, you tell the viewer what you want them to do right away. Obviously, you won't do this with your literal first words but a short introduction followed by a soft CTA is a great option for these ads.

From an advertising point of view, these ads are perfect since you only pay if a viewer clicks on the ad link or if they watch the video past thirty seconds. In either case, you're paying for real engagement and what's more, the viewer has prequalified themselves by making the effort to engage with you. For someone to put their preferred video on hold and check out your stuff on the back of a five to ten second preview, they probably have high levels of curiosity.

The best part of all this is that your audience preselects itself, and you also get the benefit of a wide reach. YouTube takes Google search history into account when someone searches for stuff on their platform, so you're able to leverage both platforms at once. From a retargeting perspective, if you choose to display YouTube ads to someone who has just visited your website, choose this format since it's a light touch and you won't be bashing your customer's head in with your product.

A variation of this ad is the one that plays in stream. This refers to when a skippable ad plays in the middle or at some other part of the video. These types of ads have lower engagement but tend to bring higher quality clicks. The reason for this is easy to understand. By the time your ad plays, the viewer has invested in the video and if they click your ad, there must be something amazing they've found with your product. Having said that, these are a minor annoyance so minimize this sort of advertising. with both the instream and the ad that plays at the start, the maximum run time is three minutes. Generally, you'll find these ads running for around half a minute at the most.

TrueView Discovery

These ads are like Google ads except they show up in the search results page on YouTube or on the homepage. There is no time limit with these ads. You will pay per click and this format of ad also has high levels of engagement since a user voluntarily chose to click on your ad.

You will need to come up with attractive copy for these ads since you will have to describe what your product is about so use one of the copywriting templates I listed earlier. A before/after/solution framework often works wonders with these types of ads.

Off late, Google has introduced a new type of ad called TrueView for reach. This type of campaign helps you get the word out to the highest number of people, and you will be paying on a CPM basis. In other words, you'll pay on the basis of how many times your video was viewed.

For the large majority of advertisers, this is not going to work. It's a bit like Facebook charging you every time your ad was shown instead of clicked. If you are a huge advertiser this might work for you since brand awareness is a big differentiator in competition. However, for small advertisers your primary goal is to convince the customer that your product is good, not why your product is better than your competitor's.

There's a subtle difference in the two approaches, which you will appreciate once you grow your business. For now, stay away from this type of campaign.

Non Skippable Ads

The fact that YouTube doesn't have a fancy marketing name for these is perhaps the best indicator as to how terrible they are for everyone involved. Still some marketers persist in using these ads, especially at the start of their videos. There's a special circle of hell reserved for such people.

Anyway, if you feel confident enough that your targeting is sound and if you have enough experience you can risk this type of ad. Why on earth you would want to invest in such ads is beyond me though.

For starters, you'll be paying on a CPM basis. So, not only will you be annoying people watching, you'll also be paying for the privilege of annoying them. You can choose to play these pre roll (before the video) or mid roll (in between) but it makes no difference, the outcome is the same.

There are very few channels out there who opt to allow ads, skippable or non-skippable, mid roll so there isn't a clear view on how exactly you'll be able to justify the expenditure on creating these things. The only people who benefit from these are large brands. Think Apple prior to releasing a new iWhatever playing a quick ten second ad to let you know that they're coming for your wallet again.

For smaller advertisers, these just aren't worth it.

Bumper Ads

These were one of the first innovations that YouTube came up with to address advertisers' outcry against the platform. To their credit, it does work to an extent. Bumper ads are around six seconds in length and are far less annoying than non-skippable ads. Another huge factor in their success is that they play at the end of the video.

Against these positives is the fact that you're still paying on a CPM basis. There's a good reason for this. If any ad network is confident of its formats and structure working, they'll charge you on a CPA basis because they know you'll keep coming back thanks to the relevance of the ROI you see. Paying on a CPM basis is the same as placing an ad in a magazine or newspaper. If you're going to pay CPM for your ads, you might as well advertise in a publication (digital or otherwise) instead of wasting time doing this.

Consider this: One of the most popular niches on YouTube is gaming. Yet, you hardly see any major video game ads beyond the usual suspects such as EA, Bethesda and so on who are behemoths of the industry. The large majority of indie and mini studio game creators advertise in publications and in places like Twitch or Steam (Lovato, 2019).

My point is that you should beware of CPM ads. They're only worth it when brand awareness becomes the biggest driver of your sales. Think of it this way: Mercedes Benz doesn't need to convince people that their cars are good. They need to convince them that they're more stylish and swag worthy than BMW and Audi. Small advertisers are never in such positions where their brands have such huge awareness. Apple versus Samsung is another good example of this.

Other Formats

Aside from video ads, YouTube also gives you the choice of overlay text ads, which are a textual overlay in the middle of videos and sponsored cards, which are small expandable cards that show up at the end of the video.

Both of these are good choices for remarketing campaigns since they're unobtrusive and don't impede the viewing experience. The ROI you'll receive depends on your niche and targeting. Generally, save all forms of YouTube marketing for remarketing efforts. This way, you'll know that you have an audience already and that from here on out it's just a matter of reminding them of their prior actions as opposed to convincing them to take a new action.

Tips to Make YouTube Work

So, is it still worth it to go on YouTube? Well, if you're releasing content on there you might as well try to advertise is what I say. Again, I want to make it very clear: for SEO and organic traffic, YouTube is fantastic. For paid search, it is the exact opposite. The platform is currently optimized for brand awareness more than anything else, so a CPA campaign is not going to get huge results.

However, you can use it to drive engagement to your existing channel and then focus on marketing to your subscribers to drive sales. This should be defined as part of your overall content strategy. If you're releasing content on your blog as well as on YouTube, then developing a synergy between the two should be easy.

Once someone visits your website, via paid search, remarket to them by setting up a campaign on YouTube. Odds are that if the viewer has good potential for a sale, they will check out your YouTube channel and will browse a few videos. You can track engagement via your dashboard and change the frequency of your ads. Needless to say always opt for skippable ads and only pay on a CTA or on a click basis. This way, you stand a good chance of getting free marketing thanks to brand recall.

A pro tip is to organize your playlists in an intuitive and easily understandable manner. Remember that a large majority of YouTube browsers tend to be on mobile. The mobile format displays playlists differently than on desktop where every playlist gets equal importance. On mobile, though, only one playlist gets importance and people have to scroll down to see more. So pick your primary playlist to highlight wisely.

Other than that, there isn't much else to paid marketing on YouTube. Simply focus on pumping out great content and focus on building your subscriber base. As you do this, you'll often find that paid search is a better option and YouTube will drive a lot of organic views to your website or blog.

Chapter 10: Getting Started as an AdWords Expert

Given the ubiquitous nature of Google ads, you'd think that every business owner out there is working with an agency or has already hired a specialist to work for them. This is actually not the true picture. Sure, the Wild West days when large brands used to manage things in-house in a hit or miss fashion are long gone, but there are a number of businesses that need AdWords help.

Becoming a Google Ads specialist is a fantastic career choice, and it enables you to join one of the fastest growing career paths out there. Digital marketing is still in its infancy, and there's a lot of room to grow. The best part is that it is mature enough for you to know that there's definite demand yet small enough for you get in at the bottom of something good.

In this chapter, I'm going to give you a brief guide on how to get started as either a freelance Google Ads specialist or how you can work for an agency.

First Steps

The first question you should ask yourself is whether you'll be a good fit to become a Google Ads professional. Here's the thing: a lot of the pioneers who are now founders of digital marketing agencies have a math or financial background. This doesn't mean you need to have worked in a bank or that you need to have an engineering degree. Far from it.

What it does mean is that you need to be comfortable analyzing mountains of data in spreadsheets and slicing and dicing that data. Unlike traditional marketing, Google Ads is not about psychology. Sure, there is a part that it plays like in everything else, but successful Google Ads campaigns are more science than art.

So ask yourself if you're comfortable drilling deep into data filled spreadsheets and whether spending the entire day looking at numbers and tweaking things again and again sounds like a wonderful time. The truth is that you need to love doing this to be successful at it. Having a quantitative bent of mind certainly helps.

Certifications

Before getting into certifications, it is important to take a step back and look at the world of online marketing. Within the Google relevant space, there are two types of marketing you can carry out: PPC and SEO. SEO is a different world even if it shares the same roots as PPC. If you are going to become a professional in Google Ads, consider an SEO certification as well since this will give you well rounded knowledge.

The other thing you need to consider is whether you want to specialize in any other platform such as Facebook, which is a worthy rival to Google's ad network. Ultimately, it comes down to what your goal is. In the beginning, it is far better to go deep than to aim for breadth. Specialize on one particular network and then upgrade your skills on others.

With this in mind, map out your planned career path. Popular goals to aim for are to join a digital marketing agency or to work as a freelancer. To be honest, working with an agency is a far better bet since you'll be able to learn a lot in very little time, plus you'll be in an environment where you'll be surrounded by people who are like-minded.

Working as a freelancer is great in that you can set your own hours, but it can be difficult to stay up to date with things. If you're coming into this field from a completely unrelated one, developing a network is going to be difficult. Ultimately, your network will land you clients, so you'll have to spend a lot of effort and energy on building these up.

This doesn't mean you won't succeed as a freelancer, but having agency experience gives you credibility plus a network to lean on. Not to mention you can start freelancing as a side hustle and then move when your income is stable. Either way, see what path suits you best and work toward that.

So, what certifications do you need? Happily, you don't need a college degree to get certified in Google Ads. Google themselves offer an AdWords course that involves hours upon hours of video lessons. These lessons are completely free and at the end of the course are two exams that you need to pass (Sauer, 2019).

The first exam will deal with AdWords fundamentals and the next one will deal with supplemental certifications. There are five supplements:

1. Shopping advertising

2. Search advertising

3. Display advertising

4. Mobile advertising

5. Video advertising

Each exam costs $50, so your total expenses on your education are $100. Pretty neat! Once you're done with your AdWords certification, Google will allow you to display the certification badge on your website and on your professional profiles on LinkedIn and such websites.

Every single Google Ads professional is Google certified these days, so this is a minimum requirement for you to possess (Sauer, 2019). Next, you need to work on your SEO certification. Here, things are a bit trickier. Google does not offer an SEO program since offering one would be akin to letting you in on the secrets of its algorithm. Hence, you need to go with a third party provider.

The thing with SEO is that it is an ever changing beast, so surrounding yourself in a good community is just as important as the training you receive. This is why you should consider joining a program that offers such benefits. Such programs will be paid, but they will pay for themselves over time. A good example of this is The SEO Playbook which costs $497.

Another good example is the SEO Training Course by Moz, which has a variable cost depending on your needs but can go as high as $600. Both of these courses will teach you to land clients quickly and network with other SEO professionals. Do not underestimate the power of your network since this will help you land clients and provide handy references in case anyone asks.

Within the free options Hubspot offers a great crash course, but the best one hands down is offered by SEMRush. This course is highly detailed and is regularly updated, so check it out if you don't have the inclination to invest.

Either way, get yourself certified in both areas. Once this is done, you can move onto the next step.

Landing Clients

The first thing you need to land clients is a website. I mean, you're advertising stuff on the web so how can you not have a website? As you're working through your certifications, build out your LinkedIn profile and begin connecting with people on there.

If you've never done this before, you'll be surprised at how willing people are to accept connection requests from those they don't know. A good way to build social proof on LinkedIn is to get above 500 connections as soon as possible. This way, people will see that you're not some lone wolf type of person who they don't know.

The easiest way to do this is to search for LIONs or LinkedIn Open Networker. These people accept invitations from anyone and everyone and usually have networks of over 10,000 people. Once you've connected with them, fire off requests to anyone who seems like a fit. Remember, the idea is to grow to 500 as quickly as possible.

As you're doing this, keep seeking out people relevant to your field. A good way to do this is to search for people with the words "digital marketing specialist" or "digital marketer" in their job titles. Connecting to content strategists is also a good idea. Also connect with people who own and operate digital marketing agencies.

You can send an introductory message with your request using the "add note" feature. Simply write that you're getting started in the field and would love to connect with them online and that's it. Don't ask for a job or anything else. Once they accept your request, send them the note again with some more details such as which industry you're looking to specialize in and such and thank them for connecting with you.

Never ever ask for a gig or a job at this stage since it's just desperate. As you complete your certification, join groups and write posts and articles on your LinkedIn profile to establish some credibility. You don't need to come across as an expert. A good way of approaching this is to ask a question in your article and try to work your way toward an answer. When writing the article, ask questions of the people you've networked with and then quote them in it.

Once the article is published, notify them of it and thank them for their help. This is a great way to get your name out there. Once your certifications are complete, it's time to actively look for jobs and the best place to start is with those you've networked with. However, do not ask them directly. Instead, write a post about it and let them see it via their updates.

Simultaneously, look for jobs on LinkedIn and sign up for Profinder. Profinder is available only in the United States and this is a great way for freelancers to build their client base. Meanwhile, start sending out emails to people who make hiring decisions in digital marketing agencies. How do you do this?

Cold Emailing Tricks

Cold emails are perhaps the biggest generator of business results for freelancers. Here's how you go about it. First, search for the appropriate job titles of people in companies you want to work for. So you can search for either the CEO or Founders of a small agency or the head of recruitment at a bigger agency or another marketing specialist who works there.

Send a request to connect with them on LinkedIn. Next, head over to their company's website and note the domain. Once this is done, head over to Hunter.io and paste the domain name and the person's name into the appropriate fields. Hunter is a great tool that will give you the email address of the person who works in that company. Every company has a certain format and this tool will help you figure out what that format is.

Once you have the email, it's simply a question of sending them an introductory email pitching your skills and what it is you're looking for. If it's a job, highlight your skills and point them to articles you've written. If you're looking for a freelancing gig, target content managers and highlight your past results.

A powerful extension you can add within Gmail is Bananatag. This allows you to track whether someone has opened your email or not. Furthermore, it allows you to delay sending the email. Mondays and Fridays are statistically the worst days for your emails to be read (Ellering, 2019). So bulk schedule your emails between Tuesdays and Thursdays.

Figure out your email template and then copy paste the appropriate information and mash that send button. Aim to send out at least twenty cold emails per day. That's twenty per five working days which works out to 100 per week. You'll schedule these 100 to be sent within Tuesday to Thursday.

Maintain a spreadsheet of who you've sent emails to and track who has opened and read your email using Bananatag, which will send you a notification within Gmail. After a week of sending your preliminary emails, send a one line follow up to those who opened your email asking them whether they would like to discuss your proposal further or not.

Following up is extremely important. Remember, these are busy people and they might have had other things to deal with instead of responding to your mail. Sending a simple follow-up allows you to remind them gently. Often, you won't get a response within a week but you might receive one many months down the line! You don't control this so focus on networking and sending as many cold emails as possible.

At some point of doing this at such a pace, LinkedIn is going to limit your usage and try to force you to convert to a paid plan. Ignore this and simply take it easy for a week or two and then get back to your usual pace. Combine this approach with attending any industry networking events, and you'll land a job in no time.

Freelancers are best served by having a proven track record to show, which is why agency experience is great since this gives you testimonials and references even if you don't have clients as yet. So consider working at an agency for at least a year before deciding to go out on your own. Remember that the agency will take care of all the marketing and advertising that you will need to do by yourself if you're a freelancer.

Salaries

On average, a Google Ads expert at the 25th percentile earns around $35,000 per year and someone in the 95th percentile will earn close to $100,000 per year (Sauer, 2019). There's a wide band here, but this is reflective of the immaturity of the space. Also, a lot depends on the location you're in.

Either way, this is a highly paid field. Freelancers on Upwork earn close to $90 per hour for their expertise (Sauer, 2019).

Conclusion

Google Ads are a fantastic and compulsory way to grow your business. Remember that your online presence is critical for your brand's perception, and Google Ads is a great way to hone this. Best of all, paid advertising helps you get the word out about yourself and the increased traffic, when well directed, will help your SEO efforts.

There is no direct link between the two in Google's algorithm, but you can bet that a person who has found you through an ad and has found your services valuable will keep coming back for more unprompted. There is a steep learning curve to success with PPC ads, but follow the simple steps outlined in this book and you'll meet with success. Best of all, PPC advertising is a completely merit based field and a small business can go toe to toe with the big boys.

The key is to not get overly smart about it and to aim to provide quality across all levels. Quality manifests as relevancy between your ads and your landing page and in the product or service you're selling. Aim for value and your Q scores and relevancy will take care of themselves.

At the heart of all great campaigns is constant testing and tweaking. To be successful with PPC, you need to constantly search and maximize your edge and |this involves trying out new things all the time. Google helps you do this with mature campaigns, but remember to split test your initial ad sets as well so that you can maximize your conversions.

Your ad is merely a gateway to your landing page so ensure your copy and design flows smoothly and sells your product honestly.

Clutter and confusion are common reasons for bounces, and you will be penalized for this. Getting a certification for Google Ads is a great way to enhance your knowledge and you can choose to build your own brand, work for an agency, or work as a freelancer once this is done.

Remember that the internet and digital media is still growing and that the sky's the limit!

I wish you all the luck in the world with your PPC journey. Happy advertising!

Printed in Great Britain
by Amazon